Stories from the Shenandoah

By Tammy Cullers and Retta Lilliendahl

Other books in the Local Lore Series:

Regards to Broadway: The Story of an American Town

Local Lore of the Shenandoah

Local Lore of the Shenandoah

Copyright © 2019 by Cullers and Lilliendahl

All rights reserved. No part of this book may be used or reproduced by any means, graphic, electronic, or mechanical, including photocopying, recording, taping, or by any information storage retrieval system without the written permission of the publisher except in the case of brief quotations embodied in critical articles and reviews.

Acknowledgments from Retta:

I want to thank each one who graciously allowed me to interview them and trusted me to write and share their stories.

Sarah Lilliendahl, who faithfully edited my writing with corrections and suggestions that added clarity to my work.

Al C. Lilliendahl, our graphic designer who designed the covers for all three books and used his magic to restore old photos.

Al S. Lilliendahl, my husband, who endured my rambling, refused to accept my writer's block, and allowed me to place my writing ahead of housework.

To all my family and friends who encouraged and believed in me along the way.

Thanks to Larry Gray, owner of the land where the spring house is located.

To the kind people who gave me referrals and shared relevant information for my fillers:

Maretta Crider, Tacy Hawkins, Brenda Whitmore, Lisa Shoemaker, Vallee Burgess, Leroy Wetzel, Jane Garrett, Merritta Kaplinger, Meredith Moore La Freniere, Frank and Ellie Mitchell, Patty Mongold, Dale MacAllister and any whom I may have forgotten.

Tammy's Acknowledgements

Writing is never a solo adventure. I'd like to thank all of those who came along on this journey, including, but not limited to:

--My husband, Randy, for always believing in me and never doubting that my crazy schemes will work out.

--The folks I've interviewed for their patience and availability and for sharing their most presious possessions: their stories.

-- My co-writer, Retta, for her patience and hard work.

--For all who editied, coached, shared, cheered, and waitied patiently for this project to be finished.

Contents

Forward	*13*
Carl and Nancy Hoover	*14*
Alma Fulk Conley	*18*
Bill and Ethel Miller	*20*
Vallie Virginia Burruss	*22*
Evelyn Moyers Rhodes	*24*
Helen Suter	*27*
Anna Magaret Fulk Cook	*29*
Mark (Babe) Armentrout/Catherine	*31*
Mary "Peggy" Reid	*33*
Amarylas Jane (Hoover) Garrett	*35*
Dorothy Jane Stone	*38*
Jack Lindamood	*40*
Annie Annie Over	*41*
History of Pepsi-Cola	*42*
Marium (Crider) Selke	*44*

Donald and Arlene Bare	47
Ethel Geil Rhodes	50
Nell Alger	52
History of Ironing	55
Richard Cullers	58
JoAnn "Cromer" Gordon	61
Hilda Rhodes	63
Mildred Kennedy Cromer	65
The Old Men of Timberville	67
Norvell Preston Trumbo, Jr. 1923-2009	69
Tom and Dorothy Hawkins Moore	72
Wild Bill Elliott	74
Frank and Ellie Mitchell	75
The Rug Shop at Chimney Rock	76
Lawrence and Linda Wilt	81
Iron Furnaces	83

Lura Ritchie	*86*
Vallie May Stroop	*88*
Harry Long	*90*
Odessa Dove Lantz	*92*
The Longest Call	*93*
Charles Moubry	*94*
Memories of Anna Harper	*96*
Jon Gordon Smith	*98*
Larry Dickinson	*100*
Day Lantz	*103*
Bea Reedy Fulk	*105*
Mutual Cold Storage	*107*
Judy Spahr	*109*
Jim Branner	*112*
Ruby Ennis	*114*
Susan Brown	*116*
Antique Cars and Trucks	*118*

Kaye Dickinson Hill   *123*

Broadway United Methodist Church   *125*

The Doc Dove House   *126*

Martha Crider Henderson   *127*

Winky Dink and You   *129*

Take Me Out to the Ballgame!   *131*

Retta Cooper Lilliendahl   *132*

Tammy Fulk Cullers   *136*

World War II Observation Tower   *139*

Jump on the Bandwagon   *140*

The Outdoor Shop   *141*

Conclusion   *143*

Forward

My grandmother was born in 1899 – the year the word "automobile" was first officially used in a New York Times article. It seems almost impossible to believe that one generation ago, cars were just being introduced to the country. Think how much has changed since then!

Nineteenth-century New England writer, Nathaniel Hawthorne, said that "time flies over us, but leaves its shadow behind." Even though technology has altered our world almost beyond comprehension, the shadow of how folks used to live still lingers. Farmers still till the land, musicians still serenade us with their songs, and folks still share stories.

In this collection of local lore, we have gathered tales from around our local towns: stories of how your neighbors persisted through the devastation of The Great Depression, the tragedy of war, and the trials of everyday life that are not so different than what we face today. People still help each other get through tough times; communities still stick together.

We have also added a few memories– reminiscences of folks who have passed on but whose memories are still with us. We hope you enjoy the stories, and we hope you realize the importance of sharing the memorable events of your own life with your family and friends.

--Tammy Cullers 2019

Carl and Nancy Hoover

The first five children in Nancy's family were all under six years old. As the second child, Nancy was aware that her mother was overwhelmed. In the 1930s, jobs were scarce and a young girl could work as a mother's helper for as low as five dollars a week. Nancy tells of a special walk they took with such a hired girl. That day the doctor arrived followed by the hired girl who promptly gathered the children and took them for a walk. Nancy said, "This event was quite unusual in itself. Country folk didn't take walks, especially with no destination in mind." Nancy's younger sister, Phoebe, who was sometimes intuitive beyond her years, whispered to her, "Do you think Mother is going to have another baby?" Nancy replied, "Of course not!" Though she really didn't have a clue. Back then, no one ever mentioned women being pregnant and the ladies wore "house dresses" that were not revealing especially to naive children. But sure enough when they were allowed back into the house, there was a new baby!

It was always a welcomed trip to the doctor's office for a few members of their little brood. As soon as they arrived in the waiting room they would snag available copies of the National Geographic Magazine and scour the pages for naked women. She shrugged her shoulders and said, "I guess it was like our little anatomy addiction."

Her oldest sister, Lois, adapted to the role of mother's helper and was relied on heavily though she was just a little girl herself. At one point her mother tried to assign two younger siblings to Nancy and her sister, Phoebe. Nancy said, "I was only eight and supposed to watch a little brother not much younger than I was. We were just too close in age and, consequently, this plan fell apart before it began.

They were always squabbling about something. The three oldest girls shared a lunchbox. On the way home from school, Nancy and Phoebe got into a royal fight about whose turn it was to carry the lunchbox while Lois walked on ahead. With no resolution, the little girls left it in the middle of the road. A short time later Phoebe went back to retrieve it. Alas, it was too late, because a car had driven over it and left it squashed.

Because Nancy lived far from school she could not stay for most of the clubs but she was able to join the Home Economics Club since it met during school hours. She was thrilled to be chosen to be an officer and invited to represent her club at an event at Bridgewater High School. When she confided in the teacher that she had no transportation to the school she was informed that if she could get to Cootes Store by a certain time she could catch a ride. At home, Nancy asked her mother how she could get to Cootes Store, and her mother's advice was, "Well, just start walking early and someone will pick you up." This was a big day for her and she was so proud reflecting on the special event as she began her walk. After over an hour with no offers, she was relieved when a man with a truck full of straw stopped. She climbed into the back with the straw and by the time she arrived at Cootes Store she was a sight. Pieces of straw were stuck in her hair, clinging to her clothing and even in her socks; nothing like the tidy little girl who had left the house. And that was how she arrived at the event as the official representative of the Home Economics Club.

Nancy was only sixteen when she married Carl Hoover, who was twenty-one. He was soon drafted into the Army and they headed to Texas where he would be stationed. A year and a half later Nancy was expecting their first child. When the baby was due, Nancy's mother, Goldie May, and sister, Lois, took the bus from Virginia to Texas in the summer heat to be with her. When Nancy went into labor, she headed for the hospital which was just across the street but labor was not productive. After seventeen hours, she overheard her mother in the hallway telling the Army doctor and the nurses that they needed to change Nancy's position and help push the baby out. They followed Goldie's instructions and baby Craig was born.

After Carl's military service, they returned to Virginia to live with Carl's maternal grandmother. She had helped raise him from when he was only three and his mother had died; and now she was a widow in need of assistance. For Nancy it was a culture shock after experiencing the modern conveniences of an indoor bathroom and more modern appliances in the Army housing. Returning with a baby in diapers she now faced a situation of no hot water, an outhouse, an old washing machine that ran by gas and a clothesline.

Carl was hired by the Broadway Post Office where he would spend the next thirty-four years. Delivering mail to the Runions Creek area, he covered a fifty-two-mile route each work day. When he started, postage was just three cents for first class and a Christmas card, if left unsealed, was only two cents. The event of mail delivery was the highlight of the day for many children who were isolated in their mountain homes. They would come running to meet Carl and often tried to climb onto the car before it had come to a complete stop. His job was also complicated by the fact that all the addresses were simply a person's name and route number. Most roads were not named at that time. And there were rarely any return addresses on the mail. Often three generations of the same family lived nearby with duplicate names and as Carl put it, "You almost had to know what they had for breakfast to figure out who it belonged to." Sometimes the mystery of the recipient was resolved by someone recognizing the handwriting or the town printed in the post office stamp. Many residents were discovering the convenience of mail ordering through a catalog. One customer complained that his wife ordered from "Sears and Send-back" instead of "Sears and Roebuck" because she often ended up returning her orders.

Nancy's first job outside of the home was at C. C. Turner's hatchery. She was taught to pick up three or four baby chicks at a time, squeeze gently till their eyes opened and dispense a drop of vaccine into each eye. Once, she rode along to deliver a large order of baby chicks, called "peeps," to a place in Petersburg, West Virginia, over a two-hour drive on old roads. She still recalls the sound of the peeps was almost unbearable.

  A decision to go to beauty school changed Nancy's life. After graduating, she began a career that connected her with the community in a personal way. Initially, she felt she could not charge the dollar and a quarter that experienced hairdressers charged for haircuts, so she only charged seventy-five cents. She was still learning to have confidence in her work and build up a client base. In the late 1960s, longer hairstyles for men brought an increase of male customers who were more comfortable with a woman styling their hair than their barbers. Nancy's business grew and when she retired after thirty-three years, the friendships she had made continued.

Alma Fulk Conley

Alma's father, Clory Fulk, raised poultry and Alma remembers an interesting home remedy that he used on the farm. When a chicken developed a cough, her dad immediately filled a sack with snuff dust and twisted the top of the sack tightly closed. Then someone, usually Alma, was given the daily chore of carrying it through the chicken houses, swinging it back and forth around each stove. It was a messy task which created a "fog" that covered her clothing, face, hands and arms. If she blew her nose afterwards, it produced a yucky brown residue.

Ralph Conley was a handsome young man with dark wavy hair who grew up in the area and attended Alma's church. He had served in the Navy and was ready to settle down. Alma was part of a large family and learned to cook, bake, and keep house at a young age. Her work included many responsibilities often assigned to men. She regularly carried a one-hundred-pound bag of chicken feed to the chicken house.

She was only fifteen when Ralph asked her to marry him, and she knew her parents would not agree, so they made plans to elope. She left a note in her bedroom one night and they went to register in Hagerstown, Maryland on a Friday. There was no blood test required and they could be married in forty-eight hours. She stayed at a relative's house until Monday when the office was open again. After they were married, they lived in Ralph's parent's home until they found a place of their own.

The first time Alma went back home for a visit she wasn't sure how her parents would react. As she was walking through the orchard she paused under an apple tree. Alma was surprised when she heard her father's voice calling her name from up in the tree. She knew by his tone that he was not angry but instead was happy to see her. She said, "It was like a burden lifted from my shoulders."

A year and a half later their daughter, Wilma Lee, was born, the first of four children. Wilma was named after Wilma Lee Cooper, a popular bluegrass-country singer, and musician of that time.

Alma recalls that when the news got out that she had gotten married so young, there were unkind remarks like, "It will never last," but Alma said, "I married for keeps!" And so she did. They had fifty-five years together before Ralph passed away.

Trovillo "Bill" and Ethel Miller

Bill grew up in a family community with all the Miller relatives living within "shouting distance" of one another. When route numbers changed to street names, the road became "Millertown Road."

He recalls his mother, Sally, was extremely afraid of thunderstorms. When the sky would darken with an approaching storm, she would gather the children and hurry to another family member's house. As a child he thought it was a curious thing, because the relative's house was the same size as their own. Eventually, his mother found a special place inside their house that she felt comfortable as a good shelter. It was a staircase with a door on either side. They huddled there with both doors shut in that dark, quiet place where the sounds of the raging storm were muffled. After one such storm she opened the inside door and through the living room window she saw their small barn ablaze from a lightning strike. There was no one to call and nothing to do except to be grateful that it was not their house. It did nothing to allay her fear of storms.

Bill worked on Mr. Zigler's farms and orchard. He operated the sprayer truck and recalls spraying for locusts that were so thick at one point that he could not see ahead of him.

His Grandad had an apple orchard and owned a cider mill. After the prep for the cider, the leftover apple pieces called "snits," were boiled till the mixture thickened into cider apple butter. Absolutely nothing was wasted; even the cores were food for their pigs.

Ethel and Bill reflected that growing up during the depression children did not have store-bought toys. Bill recalled, "If a boy found a large stick, it was a horse to ride. An empty bottle pushed along the ground by a little hand was a car." As a young girl, Ethel had a collection of rocks which she played with as dolls. One day she went to visit her aunt nearby taking one of her rocks along. She had a younger cousin, Rita, who was enjoying a large bucket of baby chicks. They were fascinated with the "little peeps" until suddenly Rita picked up Ethel's rock and dropped it into the bucket. They were both startled when it killed one of the chicks. Ethel quickly ran home afraid that her aunt might think she dropped the rock on the chick.

Their families never wasted anything. Today they still hate to throw anything away remembering the time when there was so little that they just did without or improvised. The canning seals of that day were a sticky textured material and came in handy when someone needed to repair the sole on a worn-out shoe.

After Bill was retired he enjoyed golf. One time while playing at The Homestead golf course, there was an older gentleman in a group who came up behind him. They let him go ahead. It was obvious he had vision problems and couldn't see the flag because someone told him the location. When he hit the ball, it passed directly over the flag. After the game Bill discovered that the man was professional golfer, Sam Snead.

Samuel Jackson Snead (1912-2002)

Sam Snead, nicknamed "Slammin' Sammy" was an American professional golfer who held the position as one of the top players in the world for almost four decades. Many believed he had the "perfect swing" and if one is curious, it is recorded in all its glory on the internet. Snead won a record 82 PGA Tour events, including seven majors. In 1973 he became the oldest player to make a cut in a U.S. Open at the age of 61. In 1974 he was inducted into the World Golf Hall of Fame and received the PG Tour Lifetime Achievement Award in 1998. In 1983 at 71 years old, Sam shot a round of 60 (12-under-par) at The Homestead golf course in Hot Springs, Virginia.

Vallie Virginia Burruss

Vallee Virginia Burruss lives in the house where her maternal grandparents lived. Her favorite childhood memories took place on this property and almost exclusively centered around her Granddaddy, M. E. Miller. Her grandmother was Becky Baker Miller and when her grandparents married someone said, "You will always be well fed because you now have a 'Miller' and a 'Baker' in your family."

Her Granddaddy was a trapper and a hunter of high caliber. He knew the woods like "the back of his hand." Vallee recalled when she walked with him he never seemed to tire. One day a youngster from the neighborhood was holding a branch from a bush and he told Granddaddy that he had gotten it from the woods just days before. The gentleman replied, "Yes, I saw where you took it from."

Once he showed Vallee the spot where he shot his first rabbit. He had been eight years old and his parents had left him alone while they ran an errand. He got his daddy's rifle and headed out into the woods. He shot the rabbit, skinned it, and had it in the pot cooking when they arrived home.

Each year on August 15 Granddaddy went squirrel hunting. Vallee smiled as she recounted, "It wasn't squirrel hunting season, but he had his 'own' season." Vallee said you could sit in the house and count the shots fired and that would be the number of squirrels he would bring back.

Although Vallee lived in the city of Harrisonburg, she was a country girl at heart. On any opportunity, she went to her grandparents' home. One day she convinced a friend to play hooky with her and they rode their bikes to her grandparents' house. Neither grandparent questioned why the girls were not in school. They stayed all day following Granddaddy around and thoroughly enjoying their adventure. They returned to school in time for closing and no one was the wiser.

This was an amazing accomplishment because everywhere you went there were eyes watching you. No one had to establish a "neighborhood watch" back then; it came naturally.

Vallee recalled a time she rode her bike through a red light because there were no cars around. By the time she got home, her father had been informed and he took her bike away for a while. A kid without a bike was in a pitiful situation, because it provided so much freedom back then. On a Saturday friends would often take off in the morning with a sack lunch and spend the day riding wherever they wanted as long as they were back before dusk.

As I was leaving the kitchen where the interview took place, Vallee stopped me in the narrow entryway. She led me into her living room where the fire from a wood stove added a cozy warmth to the room and a rocking chair displayed a crocheted quilt she had made. Granddaddy loved to build a roaring fire on cold days but Grandmother refused to go to bed until the last ember smoldered out. Even then, she sprinkled water over the ashes and stirred them before she was satisfied. Vallee shared that when she was a child there had been no heat upstairs and the closed in entryway between the living room and kitchen had been an open porch. By morning it was bitter cold upstairs in the bedrooms. Her grandmother rose early and started the wood stove in the kitchen and Vallee awoke to the smells of breakfast. Those winter mornings she always scurried down the stairs, through the living room, across the cold porch, and into the warm kitchen as fast as she could run.

But it was a special photo that Vallee wanted to share with me of her menfolk from the past taken at the old moonshine still. When she looks at it she has one regret. She never thought to ask her grandparents to identify those in the photo. Almost every senior has a box of old photos or letters. For those reading this, Vallee would like to encourage you to try to label any photos or old letters lying around. Future generations will be glad you did!

Evelyn Moyers Rhodes

Evelyn (Moyers) Rhodes was born in the 30's, the youngest of five children. She grew up in Frog Hollow, a name that almost always produces a smile from people who have never seen a hollow or sat on a porch listening to the serenade of frogs.

Her brother Elmer Lee was a sickly boy though Evelyn was too young to understand the extent of it. Family recalls he often carried little Evelyn on his hip. He was only fifteen years old and she was four when he passed away. It was her first great loss.

Evelyn recalls picking wild blackberries with her mother. One time after picking they left an article of clothing on the back of a wooden chair. Her Great Aunt Molly stopped by for a visit and sat in the chair. The next day all three of them suffered from exposure to "chiggers". Chiggers are also called "red bugs" but they are not bugs or insects. They are a larval stage of a type of mite. These critters use their mouths to drill tiny holes into the skin secreting special salivary enzymes into the skin which breaks down the skin cells and cause an intense itching sensation that can last for many days.

One spring when she was about ten, Frog Hallow experienced a flood. Her daddy came to school to get her and take her home by horseback. The poor, old horse was blind and the water was up to its stomach. The animal was so frightened it kept heading toward deeper water. Her brother Harold appeared on the other side of the water and repeatedly called to the horse and it finally followed his voice out of the flooded area. Harold told her years later that if he had not been there, he hated to think what might have happened.

As a child she remembers making a playhouse out of a manure spreader, off season, of course. She used two empty orange crates for her furniture. One sat upright for her icebox and the other was upside down on the ground for her stove.

At eleven years old Evelyn was devastated when her father died suddenly. She was "Daddy's Girl" and loved to follow him around the farm while he was working.

The funeral was held at Mount Zion Brethren Church where construction had been in progress to dig out underneath the church to add a basement. The mourners filled the building and many stood outside. The weight of all the mourners caused the floor to settle but fortunately the furnace kept the floor from falling into the space below.

At the funeral there were young girls chosen as "flower girls" who carried bunches of long-stemmed flowers tied with pretty ribbons. At the cemetery the girls placed them on the closed coffin. It was a touching moment that Evelyn never forgot.

Two years later the family would return to the little cemetery beside the same country church to commit her mother to rest after just a few days of illness. Evelyn moved in with siblings until she married.

Evelyn met her husband Donald Rhodes when she was sixteen on a blind date at church. When they married two years later they rented a little house and it was the first time Evelyn had the luxury of a home with indoor plumbing.

They were blessed with four children and moved several times as the family grew. In 1963 they bought their first house where Evelyn still resides. Sadly, Donald died just short of his fifty-third birthday.

Evelyn's faith in God sustained her and she turned to childcare to provide for her own children. She is thankful for growing up in a special place like Frog Hollow and for all who have been part of her life. Greatly loved by family and friends alike, she is called "Mama Evelyn" by her church family.

This is a recent photo of the spring house in Frog Hollow that straddles a branch of Joe's Creek on land belonging to Larry Gray.

Helen Suter

Before Helen's family moved to Harrisonburg, they lived in Selma, Virginia. A favorite pastime in Selma was square dancing led by her father, John Warlitner, who was an excellent Caller for the dance steps. But when they arrived in Harrisonburg, the residents were not familiar with this type of dance, so her dad introduced it.

In anticipation of a square dance at their home, Helen's mother, Alice, would prepare several special desserts for the event. On those Sunday afternoons, they would move the large dining room table out of the way and have their collection of phonograph records ready. The old-fashioned phonograph had a crank on one side. It worked similar to the old ice cream makers. To make it operate, someone had to keep the crank turning. That's when the fun began.

Their home was a gathering place for kids and as Helen said, "Dad was the biggest kid on the block!" No matter what they were doing, he would join in and everyone enjoyed his company. Her mother never knew how many kids would still be there in the morning.

In the summer, Helen remembers biking double with a sibling to the in-ground cement pool in Keezletown to swim all day. It was about five or six miles from their home. Only two siblings from their family could attend at a time because they only had one bike.

Besides her regular job at the telephone company, Helen also drove the school bus for over twenty years. She was often asked to teach others. One day her boss informed her that she was going to teach Bill O'Brien to drive. He was the County Administrator for Rockingham County and she initially felt a little intimidated. But her boss explained that there were times the school board needed to be at a certain location and Mr. O'Brien decided he would get a bus license to eliminate the task of locating a driver.

The first time out, she purposely took him on some of the worst school routes that existed. She knew it would be important for him to know first-hand that some of the areas were treacherous. On the way, Bill asked, "Where did you find these roads?" to which she replied, "These are routes our bus drivers maneuver every day."

Then one day she told Bill to wear old clothes because he would be learning how to attach snow chains to the tires. The chains were stored inside a large box in the back of the bus. Helen kept a pair of overalls and a sheet of plastic in there, too. Her husband, Boyd Suter, had designed a wooden box and a special wooden wedge to help her with the process. She would place the sheet of plastic on the ground so she could crawl under the bus to position the box and the wedge. It was only necessary to apply chains to the outside tires of the set of back tires. Helen drove the bus onto the wooden box, which left the outside tire exposed. Next, she would fling the heavy chain on top of the tire and attach the ends. Then she would repeat the process on the opposite side of the bus. Bill was surprised that she could even lift the heavy chains. It was a strenuous job, especially adding the weather factor, but every bus driver understood it was just part of the job.

Anna Magaret Fulk Cook

Anna Margaret grew up in the small community of Cootes Store. Today her elementary schoolhouse with its vacant bell tower still stands on a hill but is now surrounded by acres of salvaged vehicles. The *current owner of the land was kind enough to have an employee walk us through the building which is now used for storage.

Childhood memories flowed as Anna Margaret walked back through time where as a little girl she learned to read, write, and discover facts about the world around her. She identified each classroom and named the teacher who taught there. Only an outline on the wall remained where a familiar blackboard had been. Pausing at a window, she described two large trees which are no longer there. Of course, the view of the mountains remained as that stable backdrop from her past. Anna Margaret sighed as she walked through the dusty rooms where there was now a car part for every piece of chalk that had been used. It was a cool fall day and reminded her that it was a cold, drafty building in its prime and only the child lucky enough to be closest to the stove was comfortable in the winter. She smiled as she pointed out one window and informed us the boys' outhouse was that direction, the girls the opposite.

By car we traced her daily walk from the school to her home. Anna Margaret stopped me partway and we got out. She pointed to a small building. One day as a child of seven, she was walking home from school. Unknown to her, her mother and grandmother were preparing for an oyster dinner event in that building. She was pleasantly surprised to hear her mother's voice calling from across the street, "Come on with us." Impulsively, Anna Margaret ran toward her mother without looking. Her teacher, though driving slowly, could not stop in time. Anna Margaret was unaware of being hit. When she opened her eyes, she heard ladies crying.

She was badly bruised and had a chipped front tooth but fortunately no broken bones.

She currently lives in the house diagonally across the street from where her maternal grandparents, Tom and Lula Hoover, had lived and where she spent most of her childhood. Her grandmother had a unique expression when she summoned Grandfather. She would step outside and call, "Ah Tom" until he responded. Anna Margaret remembers when her great aunt wrote a letter to her grandmother, it began with "Dear Aunt Lu and Ah Tom."

In the spring her granddaddy would take the cattle up on the mountain to an area he owned so they could graze. He would leave them there checking on them regularly until fall when he would bring them home again. Sometimes he would return with wild grapes so Grandmother could make a pie. He loved grape pie. Another favorite food of her grandfather's was "old black apple butter." It was apple butter made with apple cider and simmered to a dark ebony hue. Anna Margaret and her grandmother preferred the more traditional recipe which they called "sugar apple butter." She was taught a little rhyme to help her stir the apple butter in the copper kettle. "Twice around the sides and once through the middle. That's how you stir the apple butter kettle."

Her home and town are filled with happy memories of her childhood.

*Thanks to Tony A. Sager, owner of **Hillside, Inc.,** for graciously opening the old school for us to tour.

Mark "Babe" Armentrout and Catherine (Phillips) Armentrout

As the youngest of six children, Mark Armentrout received the nickname, "Babe" and it stuck with him into adulthood. Babe explained, "With several other Mark Armentrouts, it was nice to have a name that identified me."

He grew up in a hard-working family that did what was necessary to make an honest buck and whenever possible help a neighbor in need. His father, Lindsey, would buy a wooded lot and proceed to clear the trees. He removed the bark to sell to the local tannery and milled the lumber in his own sawmill. The sawmill was operated by a steam engine. It was heavy and dangerous work. The steam engine needed careful monitoring and required a steady supply of wood and water. The correct water level was imperative to regulate the steam. The sawmill itself could keep three men working all day. Babe and his brothers worked with their dad, continuing the family business when he retired.

Babe served his country in the Army. When he returned he married Catherine Phillips, a friend he had known most of his life. She came to Keezeltown regularly to visit her grandmother who lived there. Later Babe's brother married Catherine's sister which created an even closer bond between the families.

Catherine was from a family of twelve children, arriving somewhere in the middle. Her father, Russel, worked on his dad's large farm. They operated a market in Washington, DC. Like most families the children helped with the chores. Of all the tasks, doing dishes was always a point of strife. The children would often squabble about whose turn it was.

One day their brother Cletus, came up with a solution. He sat down with a lined notebook and worked out a schedule. It was complicated because some of them had chores that interfered with staying after certain meals. When he finished, it became the final word for many years.

When the youngest child, Raymond, was only two and a half years old, disaster struck the Phillips family. Their father perished in an auto accident. Everyone did their part to help keep the family together. Older siblings got jobs to provide necessities. Catherine had no idea how her mother accomplished all that she did to provide for the family. She recalls that her mother made sure all the children were fed before she ate.

Adjustments had to be made to the chore notebook as older siblings began to work away from the home, but it was still their guidebook for "Who's washing? Who's drying?" and so on. One day when little Raymond was old enough to notice the book discussion, he asked, "Where is MY name?" Then someone explained "This book was made before you were born." This made little Raymond cry, much to the amusement of the older children who understood the book's significance.

Photo of the old steam engine with Babe and Catherine's daughter, Phyllis.

Mary "Peggy" Reid

    Mary "Peggy" Reid grew up on her Granddaddy's farm in the Shenandoah Valley. Her grandmother had died when Peggy's dear mother was only fifteen and she took over the housekeeping and cooking for her three brothers and father, who was Peggy's Granddaddy. He was a kind grandfather and she recalls, when he went into town for errands, he always brought back a "poke" of candy for Peggy. A "poke" is an antiquated word for a small paper bag. He had a unique habit of giving people nicknames. He gave her the nickname, Peggy, renamed her little brother, Danny, "Sam" and Peggy's younger sister Janet he called Betsy. Granddaddy also had his own peculiar way of eating an apple. On many a winter evening, Peggy recalls watching him cut an apple in half and using a knife he scraped it across the flesh of the apple producing, as it were, a raw applesauce and ate it from the knife. When he was finished all that was left was the scraped-out peel and the core.

    Peggy was very responsible and would care for her little brother and sister when her mother would leave the children with their grandfather for a short visit. She only remembers one unfortunate incident when her mother was away. Little Sam who had often watched the adults weed the garden decided to weed it by himself. Granddaddy noticed him too late after all the newly sprouted onions had been pulled.

    Her family were active members at the Linville Creek Church of the Brethren in Broadway, Virginia where she still attends. There was one very nice young man named Paul Reid who was also in the congregation. One day when Peggy was walking home from school, Paul stopped his car and offered her a ride. That was when she knew he liked her. Granddaddy liked him, too, and gave him the nickname "Joey."

Paul owned a garage that was located near the Linville Creek. Sometimes in the spring, when the creek flooded, they were forced to evacuate and bring some of the tools home until the water receded. At first, Paul repaired the trucks exclusively for the Mutual Feed Company next door but as news of his mechanical skills spread, he added other customers and eventually hired more men to work in his garage.

Paul and Peggy had three daughters and a son. Peggy was a busy mother yet still made time to be part of a program at her church called, "Women's Work" which later changed its name to Women's Fellowship. It began in the early 1950's and the ladies met monthly to plan various church activities and dinners. They decorated and prepared food for special functions and bake sales. They also extended a helping hand for those in need, often taking meals or flowers to the shut-ins. Many today would scoff at the title "Women's Work," but let's just say it was a different time.

Amarylas Jane (Hoover) Garrett

When Jane grew up in the small community of Cootes Store, Virginia, good neighbors became an extension of the family. Daisy and Zack Turner's garden ran along the edge of their yard. The children called Mrs. Turner, "Ma Daisy." Jane remembers when she and her sister, Eleanor, would see the neighbor in the yard, they would call, "Ma Daisy, can we come out?"

She usually replied, "Yes" and the sisters would walk "out" of their yard to join her. They enjoyed their time following her around and helping her, if they could. For instance, if Ma Daisy was picking beans, they would help.

There was an old cemetery located between the old Route 259 and the new road. The children spent many hours playing in and around the cemetery. The lovely woods nearby provided a good supply of fallen limbs and sticks to form "houses" on the ground there. Teaberry growing nearby became pretend food. Their "plates" were the glass tops pounded out of old zinc canning jar lids.

Not far from the cemetery was a pull off area for cars with a picnic table. She remembered special picnics where siblings or cousins would bring homemade mustard sandwiches to eat. It was an easy sandwich to make. Just two slices of bread with yellow store-bought mustard in the middle. Yummy, what wasn't to love? Just the memory of it made Jane smile.

A long building in her yard held a wash house, a section for a coal bin, a smokehouse where the hams were hung, and an open space with a covered cistern. This was the place where Jane made her mud pies. It was serious business for little girls. The dirt came from the driveway, but adding the right amount of water took practice. Jane used old zinc canning lids to form the perfect pies. One day she saw a supply of big bumble bees nearby and thought they would look nice in her pie. When an angry bee stung her on the head she decided to stick with her original recipe.

Jane's dad, Lloyd Hoover, was a man of vision. He would see a need in the community and find a way to meet it. He owned Cootes Store for many years. It was the store from which the town got its name. The original office soon became a kitchen and then the store was expanded for a restaurant. Eventually he added a two-bay garage for repairs. Lloyd bought state police cars with markings removed from the auto auctions. He would repair them to resell on his own used car lot. He also expanded the store name to Cootes Store Service Station.

By the time Jane was thirteen, she was working at the store in the summer and on Saturdays. She often walked the 3 or 4 miles to the store or caught a ride with the postal carrier. As she got older her responsibilities increased to slicing lunch meat, grinding meat, and pumping gas.

The store was a gathering place for the community. It carried punch boards, a hand-held double layered cardboard with numerous small circles. With the tip of a pencil or pen, you would push a circle through. The inside of the punched hole would reveal if you won a prize. Since it was considered gambling thus illegal in Virginia Jane was taught to be aware. When a stranger stepped inside the store she hid the card under the counter and quickly swept away any punch pieces left. The cost per punch was only a nickel and the locals enjoyed hoping for a win.

Another friendly wager occurred when two men would stop

by for a Coke and would agree to this game. They would each pick up a bottle out of the ice chest and look at the bottom. The location of the manufacturing plant was marked there. The person holding the bottle from farthest away had to pay an additional 5 cents for the other man's drink.

They sold fresh vegetable soup daily and delicious chili dogs. The chili recipe was from local Velma Reedy's original recipe and people would come from all around to buy them. The price was twenty-five cents for two chili dogs and a soft drink. Plate lunches were soon added, which included a choice of meat with two sides and a drink for seventy-five cents.

One day a young man named Warren Sherwood Garrett stopped in with his boss for lunch. This was the beginning of a special relationship. Jane and Warren were married in 1955 on Christmas Day. After his tour in the military they moved into a house just across the street from the store.

When Jane's father sold the store and service station he built a four-bay garage across the road. He opened a twenty-four-hour business called Hoover Wrecker Service. It had a variety of equipment from tow trucks to heavy duty trucks and even a rollback, a carrier that hauls multiple cars.

When Lloyd retired, he sold the wrecker service to Warren and Jane. They operated the business for a number of years. Warren bought a tractor trailer and hauled processed chicken from Timberville, Virginia to Miami, Florida and returning with fresh produce for a market in New York. When a call came in for a wrecker and the men were not available, Jane would take out the small wrecker or the rollback to pick up vehicles.

One such call came in to pick up two cars from an accident in the next town. Jane responded quickly with the rollback. When this petite lady appeared, there were a few men standing by who let her know they didn't think she could do it. Much to their surprise, Jane proceeded to load the two cars in good time.

Dorothy Jane Stone

Dorothy Stone's home, former home and office of Dr. Gilbert Ralston

When Dorothy married Brooks Hershel Stone, he told her he didn't want any dogs or cats inside the house. Dorothy was disappointed because she loved pets. But things changed when their youngest child, Debbie, came along. She was a pet lover just like Dorothy. At one point she begged for a little chihuahua. She promised to take good care of it and keep it in her bedroom upstairs, so Dorothy consented.

The secret pet plan went well until that evening when the family was sitting around the dinner table. Debbie was horrified to hear the sound of her precious Peanut's toenails clicking along the downstairs hallway. The pup entered the dining room and went directly toward Debbie's father who was seated at the head of the table. Sitting down, the pup looked up at him. Debbie's fears were quickly allayed when she saw that her father was amused. He said with a smile, "Well, where did you come from?" It was love at first sight and the two soon became good friends.

Dorothy's aunt, who was her grandmother's caregiver, passed away. So, Dorothy welcomed her one hundred-year-old grandmother, Eliza, into her home. They also took in Eliza's old calico cat. It had been an outdoor cat so they made a place for it outside initially. Then, one day Dorothy opened the door and the cat came inside and sat down. She picked it up and realized that it was very skinny; further inspection showed the poor thing had no teeth. Canned cat food was added to her diet and the cat flourished.

One evening when Dorothy arrive home from shift work, her husband told her to turn on the bedroom light. To her surprise there was the old calico cat sound asleep up against Brooks's back. Dorothy said, "Now I've seen everything, a man who didn't want animals in his house has a cat in the bed!"

Dorothy's grandmother used snuff and kept a small tin with a little snuff stick in her pocket. One day Eliza pulled out the snuff and realized her stick was gone. The next day when Dorothy was brushing Eliza's hair, much to their amusement she found the little stick tucked above Eliza's ear.

They had a problem with moles in their yard and someone suggested they plant a castor bean plant. They did and when it grew and produced beans the mole problem gradually disappeared. There is much discussion on the internet regarding whether or not this actually works, but from Dorothy's experience it was a complete success.

Close up of a Castor plant

Jack Lindamood

Jack Lindamood was born in Timberville, Virginia, the second of four sons. His father, Charles, was a good-hearted man and showed much interested in his sons' lives. Their dad was instrumental in starting the Little League team in Timberville and coached for many years. The boys loved baseball and played on the same team.

On a school field trip in the area Jack's class went to a farm where they were shown a spring house with arrowheads embedded in the outer wall. It made an impression on him and today he has an interesting collection of arrowheads, even spear heads which he purchased, and a celt. A celt is a stone about the size of a man's fist. It was given a smooth surface by hand-grinding or by using another abrasive stone. It was basically a wood-working tool which was inserted into a socketed wooden handle. Jack shared that according to one source it was also used to scrap the inside surface of hides.

Jack's grandfather owned over two-hundred acres and planted an orchard which included cherry, apple and peach trees. The orchard thrived for many years as it changed hands from from owner to owner.

The Charles Town Racetrack in West Virginia opened in December of 1933 and was an attraction not only for locals but drew interest from far and wide. Besides the track, there was a grandstand, club house, stables and everything else needed to support the business.

When the boys were old enough, they would accompany their dad to watch the splendid thoroughbreds race. Jack's dream came true as an adult when he owned a gelded bay horse, which he named "Yo Jack."

After high school Jack worked on his grandfather's farm and at the cold storage facility. He served two years in the Army then returned home. Jack found employment as inspector for the highway department and lastly worked for Rockingham Hardware for thirty-two years.

Annie Annie Over

A popular schoolyard game that began around the 1920s was known by several names: Annie Annie Over, Annie Over, Andy Over, Auntie Over, and so on. The game required just a schoolhouse with a pitched roof and a ball. Often the ball was homemade from a rolled-up rag wrapped completely around with string. The children separated into two teams, one on each side of the schoolhouse.

A player on the team possessing the ball would attempt to throw it over the schoolhouse, calling out, "Annie Over." If it fell short and rolled back, the team with the ball would shout "Pigtail!" and try again.

When the ball succeeded in clearing the roof, the team that threw the ball then proceeded to run completely around the outside of the school building, while someone on the team that caught the ball tried to hit the children coming from the other team as they passed. Anyone tagged would then be on the team that received the ball.

Then the team that caught the ball would proceed to throw it back over the roof and the game would repeat until all of the players were on the same team.

In another variation of the game, the team that caught the ball would run around to the other side of the schoolhouse, to hit or catch the players on the team that threw the ball. If the players that threw the ball made it to the other side, it was then their turn.

Although one might choose an older child who was a fast runner with a good aim to have the ball, there might be others who would pretend to have it as well. Near the end of the game, the ball might be hidden in the hand of a young child, who could tag an unsuspecting survivor.

History of Pepsi-Cola

Pepsi was birthed in 1893 in a drug store owned by Caleb Bradham in North Carolina. When Mr. Bradham mixed a concoction of sugar, water, caramel, lemon oil, nutmeg, and other natural additives he realized that it tasted swell. He named it "Brad's Drink" and offered it as a healthy beverage to combat indigestion. It was a hit with his customers, and Bradham decided to change the name to identify it better. He renamed it Pepsi which was taken from the word dyspepsia, meaning indigestion. Its slogan "Exhilarating, Invigorating, Aids Digestion" said it all.

In 1898, he renamed it Pepsi-Cola. When the Pure Food and Drug Act of 1906 was passed banning ingredients such as arsenic, lead, barium, and uranium from food and beverages,

Pepsi-Cola did not have to change a thing since it had none of these impurities. But if you wanted a bottle to drink with your burger in the privacy of your own home, you would have to wait a few years as it was only in syrup form dispensed from the soda fountain.

Once it was bottled, and franchises made it more available, the magic brew spread far and wide. Pepsi was "aiding digestion" everywhere until a slight hiccup called World War I (1914-1918) disrupted shipping and America's supply of sugar. After the war, the price of sugar soared from three cents to twenty-eight cents per pound. Bradham bought up large quantities at the high price, one factor in the company's eventual demise. Pepsi-Cola went bankrupt in 1923 and sold its assets for $30,000.

But through the years of setbacks with war and diet fads, Pepsi has survived and today is still one of the most popular colas around. And for those who grew up with it next to their burger, like the Cooper family in Massachusetts, it's still #1.

Marium (Crider) Selke

Marium recalls a special memory which occurred when she was seven. She had walked to the sawmill where her grandfather worked to tell him dinner was ready. On the way the sky darkened and as she arrived it began to pour. Grandfather quickly leaned several heavy boards against a tree that formed a lean-to. They crawled underneath and he held her in his lap till the storm passed.

The schoolhouse she attended like most in the 1920's was just one room. The blackboard spanned almost the entire length of the class room wall. Each grade was seated together by rows. There was a long bench in the front where the teacher would call one grade at a time for their lesson. The younger children would often learn arithmetic early after hearing the facts recited by the older grades.

She remembers one day just about an hour before school was finished her tooth began to throb with pain. The teacher heard her cry and sat Marium on her lap with her cheek pressed against her chest for warmth. The teacher continued with the lesson and Marium was comforted until the end of school.

As soon as they would arrive at school the teacher would choose two of the older children to go to the neighbors for water from an outside pump. They carried two buckets on a pole between them. Filling the buckets as high as they could, they walked carefully so they wouldn't spill. In the small back room of the school was a metal box with a spigot near the bottom. One of the children would open the lid and they would pour the water inside. That was the water supply for the day and they usually needed every drop.

In nice weather the children could take their lunch boxes outside to the school yard. Marium remembers sitting on the old split rail fence. There was an apple tree with branches extending over the fence. When apple season came the children would enjoy that special treat.

In the winter when the ground was covered with snow, Marium's neighbor would harness his horses to a makeshift sled. It was in fact a wagon with seats mounted on sled runners. The horses wore sleigh bells attached to their harnesses and the children were always delighted to hear the sound of the bells ringing as the horses trotted across the field. They would bundle up in their woolen clothes and run outside in anticipation of that glorious ride to school.

The cold weather also brought the excitement of Christmas preparation at school. The children made decorations for their classroom tree and practiced for their program that would be presented to family and neighbors. Every child, no matter how small, was given a part. At the completion of the program the teacher would present each child with a gift of hard candy like a peppermint stick or candy cane.

Marium's mother raised ducks, geese, and chickens. The chickens were penned as much for their safety as anything. They were raised for eggs and meat. The children learned early not to name the chickens, because if they did there would be a very sad child at the dinner table refusing to eat the main course.

There was a river bed on their homestead and it was a delight to watch the ducks and geese roam there laying their eggs in the grass along the bank. She loved to see a duck dive down into the water to retrieve a snack with its "fanny" in the air and feet paddling wildly. Baby ducklings were a constant entertainment in the spring. The geese and ducks would come into the yard twice a day for their feedings of corn. After their evening meal they would settle down in the yard for the night. The ducks were friendly but the geese were a different matter. You had to stay alert because if they felt cornered, you would get pecked.

Before leaving for school in the morning, Marium would milk the cows. When she was finished, she would strain the milk into a heavy crock, then cover the top with a clean cheesecloth and secure it tightly around the edge with strips of cloth. The milk would be left overnight for the cream to rise. Finally, in the morning she would collect the cream from the day before, pouring it into smaller metal jugs. Some of the cream was for home use but some was sold. She recalls setting it out once a week to be collected by a truck from the local creamery.

On Saturday the house was filled with mouth-watering aromas as her mother and older sister prepared desserts for the coming week. Baking with a wood stove required much skill. Keeping the oven at an even temperature took patience and experience. They would make cookies for the children's lunches and always included something special for Sunday dinner. Marium's favorites were Mother's vanilla loaf cake with delicious caramel icing and her chocolate cake with buttercream frosting.

Donald and Arlene Bare

Arlene remembers when the young people would gather at her house for a taffy pull. The house would fill with the sweet aroma of the taffy ingredients as her mother, Sally Miller, would stir the mixture in a pot on the stove. When it was cooked to the right temperature, and cooled enough to handle, the youth would take a little butter and rub it on their clean hands. This was when the fun began! Working in twos, they would very gently pull the mixture several inches and quickly fold the taffy back on itself, then one would catch the fold and pull it back again. They would repeat the process until the taffy was hard and held its shape. Then they would put it on a platter and with a sharp knife, Mother would cut it into bite-sized pieces.

Donald grew up on Little North Mountain in a family of five sons. Donald was the oldest son, and sadly the only still surviving. As a youngster, Donald had a trap line. Before school, he would milk the family cow and hurry to check his trap. On these early morning walks, he would see as many as five stills starting up. After the fires were started, the fuel would switch to chestnut wood because it didn't smoke. When he got to the trap, he might find a muskrat or even a skunk, but on the rare occasion that he spotted a mink, his heart would beat a little faster. A mink pelt would bring twenty dollars, and later on, as high as forty. The money he earned from selling the pelts bought his clothes.

One of his fondest family memories was hunting with his dad. Donald was twelve when he learned to shoot with musket loaders. In Virginia, they would hunt on state land near Staunton, but his favorite hunting trips were out West in Colorado or Montana where they would hunt antelope, elk, or mule deer.

Donald's grandfather, Brian Conley, who he called Pop, ran a sawmill and Donald helped occasionally. His job was to load the wood to fire the steam engine. Every now and then, even though there was a protective screen, the engine would emit a loud "pop" and sparks would fly around the screen. His shirt would be speckled with holes from the spray and it would feel like tiny needles burning into his skin.

His grandmother, Edith Conley, who family called Mom was an excellent cook and frequent hostess. She would set twelve places on the table three times a day and everyone knew they were welcome to stop by. One specialty of hers was called Warm Bread. She baked it in a large iron skillet in the oven. It had the consistency of biscuits, and Donald has never tasted anything like it since. She served it with their homemade butter and apple butter and some of the most amazing jams. Back in that day, they didn't use pectin, they just let it simmer until it thickened and it had a wonderful flavor. She even made a jam from tomatoes.

At sixteen, Donald heard a sermon by Evangelist Silas Brydge that would change his life. Donald had a born-again experience and ultimately dedicated his life to full-time Christian ministry. He served as Pastor for about forty years at the Hebron Mennonite Church in Fulks Run, Virginia. Today, Donald and Arlene count themselves blessed with a busy life that includes five grandchildren and four great-grandchildren.

Photo of the original Hebron Mennonite Church building used with permission from Lorie Shiflet

Ethel Geil Rhodes

It was in the second grade that Ethel encountered her first Santa Claus. He made his arrival known with a loud thud in the hallway wearing heavy boots. The children were delighted when he entered the classroom and presented each child with a treat of candy probably purchased by their teacher. Years later, she assumed that he was her teacher's brother dressed up in a Santa costume to surprise the children. Ethel explained, "Santa wasn't big back then. We didn't even have a Christmas tree in the 1930s."

In the fourth grade, Ethel had a very difficult school year. The teacher would regularly keep classmates from recess for discipline. Once she delayed the entire class after school, causing a boy to miss his bus. One fateful day, the teacher was grading Ethel's spelling assignment and she decided that the capital O in October, where Ethel had dated the paper, was too small for her liking so she marked it as a misspelled word. It seemed so unfair yet Ethel had felt too intimidated to speak up.

One day Ethel's sister, Maude, was crossing the road after getting off the school bus and a truck came from behind the bus and hit her, resulting in a broken leg. This was before the school bus laws were passed. The same fourth grade teacher who had never shown any sympathy in class sent her sister a puzzle of the United States. This act of kindness surprised Ethel and her sisters. It was a very thoughtful gift and Ethel said they all enjoyed it. She, personally, learned all the shapes of the states from that puzzle.

Ethel lived in the family home and stayed on to care for her parents in their later years. She took business courses in accounting at Madison College which led to a job in the office of Beacon Showalter Feed in Broadway, Virginia.

One day, Frank Rhodes, a widower and mutual friend of Ethel's family, invited her to have lunch at Evers Family Restaurant. They enjoyed each other's company and after a lovely courtship, they were married.

In the early 1990s, Frank and Ethel took a summer road trip to Alaska. They drove from Virginia through Michigan and across the Canadian Providences to Alaska. Ethel recalls the unique experience that, "It never got dark while we were there." On the way home, they drove south through California and across the US and stopped for a visit with each of Frank's children and grandchildren before arriving home in Virginia. It has always been a special memory for Ethel, even dearer, since Frank's passing.

Nell Alger

Nell Alger recalls spending a lot of time alone. The youngest of seven children, there was a six-year gap between her and her next older sibling. Her father owned over one hundred acres of land which included a dairy farm. She lived in her own little world and spent most of her time with the dogs and other animals. She loved horses and being an imaginative child made up a game called "Horse." It was a very simple game to play since she was the horse! Nell galloped freely around the large farm, neighing and looking at the world through the eyes of a horse.

Nell remembers when her father, John H. Alger, ordered some special glasses for the chickens. He explained to her that chickens were attracted to a sore or broken skin on other fowl, and would peck at the area which caused more damage or even death. In the late 1930s rose-colored glasses for chickens were invented. There was a theory that if you put glasses with red lenses on the chickens they would not see the bloody sores. They tried it for a while, but eventually gave up. Beside the extra expense, attaching the glasses to their noses caused problems of its own. But during that time, it produced some very intellectual-looking creatures in the chicken yard.

She will never forget that special day when she was given her very own pony, which was part Tennessee Walking Horse. He was named Patches because of his pretty markings. Nell was about ten years old when she rode Patches bareback to bring in the cows for milking. She often rode horses with her sister, Millie. One moonlit night they decided to ride up the concrete steps outside the old Broadway Elementary School auditorium/gymnasium.

One of the horses left its "calling card" during the visit. However, they didn't get into trouble because there was no one around on that beautiful evening and it still remains a special memory for her.

Nell attended Eastern Mennonite High School in Harrisonburg, Virginia, staying in the girls' dorm five days a week. A newly completed 90-foot smoke stack tower yet unused was in sight of the high school. She was commenting to her friends, the Detweiler twins, that she had shimmied up the 50-foot silo on the family farm and she assumed that she could climb this one. With the encouragement of the boys, Nell proceeded to climb it. Inside there was a ladder of sorts with rounded rungs set a bit far apart for a teenage girl's stride, but she met the challenge. When she reached the top, Nell sat on the edge to enjoy the view. Glancing down she noticed a crowd forming on the porch of the administration building.

Students were seated alphabetically during chapel which put Nell right in the front row the next day. An announcement was made that there was to be no more climbing of the smoke stack, especially by girls. The announcement did not bother her since there was no need to do it again, but the fact that the phrase "especially by girls" was added really made her angry.

In 1958 Nell traveled to Alberta, Canada to work with a Mennonite group located in a remote area. Nell led a girls' club on Saturday afternoons which often included First Nation girls from the local reservation. They would often make crafts as a way to care and connect. Nell recalls ironing clothes for the staff with a unique iron. It had an unusual cylinder on top of the handle which she filled with white gas, closed tightly, and lit it with a match.

After Nell returned from Alberta, many things had changed. Her brother Nelson had married and taken over the farm while her father and mother now lived in a new home.

Nell's mother was an animal lover just like Nell and was pleased when Nell took in two baby skunks that were descented, of course. In those days, you could have a young skunk descented and it would be a loving pet. Nell recounted "A pet skunk was a wonderful pet to have when a salesperson appeared. You sent it to the door. They never knocked twice."

Growing up Nell enjoyed hunting especially with her brother J.P. They hunted for deer, rabbit, and squirrel and used the meat for food. The largest buck she shot was nine points. She has the head mounted in her den.

Nell's father, John H. Alger, was a kind man. He was always looking for ways to help the poor. Often, he would send an older child to drive someone to the grocery store who had no vehicle. He would never accept money; it was just what a good neighbor did. During WWII he had German POWs work on the farm. He also participated in the Mennonite worker exchange program. Both men and women from Switzerland, Germany, and The Netherlands were given an opportunity to work.

Many workers spoke very little English when they arrived. Nell recalls one man coming to the house all excited saying, "The chickens are up in the high!" Approaching the chicken house, there was quite a commotion and they were surprised at the source. There was a distraught monkey in with the chickens. They soon discovered it was a pet that belonged to a neighbor's son that had gotten out.

History of Ironing

We do not know precisely when the wrinkle revolt began, but there are records dating a thousand years back that showed the Chinese ironing. They used pans filled with hot coals to press cloth.

As early as the Middle Ages, blacksmiths forged smoothing irons. These irons were known as flat irons and sad irons. (see sketch) The term "sad" was taken from an Old English word that meant solid or heavy. These irons often weighed between five and seven pounds. Irons used by tailors for heavy duty cloth could be fourteen pounds or more.

Viking graves revealed some women's coffins included round dark glass for smoothing fabric, just in case it turned out the afterlife still contained wrinkles. My guess, though unsubstantiated, is that their daughters slipped the smooters in as an excuse to be liberated from ironing day. None the less, ironing survived and almost every civilization has had their own devices. Unlike the mousetrap, there are hundreds of ways to smooth a wrinkle.

Glass smoothers with wooden handles were common in the late Middle Ages in Wales and England. Inverted mushroom-shaped smoothers made from glass, stone, and marble existed. Decorative designs were added to the handles perhaps to give flair to a task of drudgery. Other methods of ironing involved pressing fabric between boards on a screw-press or feeding damp cloth through rollers.

Another popular ironing tool that dated before the 1600s was the mangle board. It included a wooden rolling pin and a flat narrow wooden board. Material was wrapped around the rolling pin and then the board was pressed back and forth across the pin. In Scandinavia and the Netherlands, it was a classic engagement gift. In a culture where a man learned the craft of woodcarving in his youth, he would often decorate the board with symbols of love for his betrothed.

Early metal irons relied on a stove or fireplace for heating. Maintaining the proper temperature was a carefully learned skill. The iron needed to be hot enough to press but not so hot as to scorch the fabric. Some young girls were taught to hold the iron near their cheek to determine the right heat. Try not to ponder this for very long. Keeping a smooth surface on the iron, especially for starched cloth, involved maintenance like sanding or adding a very thin coating of beeswax to the iron's surface before heating. Some wealthy households had a special stove just for ironing, with indentations on top to hold several irons.

Charcoal irons had a thick iron base with a hinged lid which provided a space to hold glowing coals to keep the iron hot for more extended periods. (see sketch)

In early North America, the tradition began with Monday being wash day followed by ironing day on Tuesday. Although families had less clothing and changed less often than today, they also had more children.

It was only inevitable that a woman would improve the iron. In 1870, Mary Potts of Iowa at the age of nineteen invented an iron with a thick base but thin sides and top, filled with material that didn't conduct heat. This kept the handle cool and the base stayed hot longer. She later improved it again by adding a detachable, wooden handle, sold in sets of three irons and a handle. While the first one was in use, the second was on the stove hot and ready and the third in the heating process. This improvement eliminated wait time.

About this same time, other inventors were beginning to develop irons that were heated by gas and alcohol fuel. An article in this book recounts Nell Alger's experience in Alberta, Canada, where she first used such an iron. It had an unusual cylinder on top of the handle which she filled with white gas, closed it tightly, and lit it with a match. (See sketch) This eliminated the need for a stove, but took little imagination to realize the dangers that came with it.

Though the first electric iron was invented in 1882, it would be years before electricity would be available to every home. When it was available, it was initially only accessible for short periods in the evening. An interesting record showed that a man named Earl Richardson from Canada was influential in convincing the local electric company to provide electricity during daylight hours on Tuesday, which was ironing day!

I could not find the exact day when that fabulous material called perma-press appeared in the stores. But by the early '60s, many ironing days had been shortened by its invention.

Richard Cullers

Richard arrived early weighing slightly less than three pounds. When his parents brought him home to the Cullers's family farm, his parents had not yet acquired a bed for him. Back then, baby chicks arrived in a 24×24 box and so they placed pillows in one such box and that served briefly as the first bed for their precious baby. Since it had been many years since a baby had grown up on the farm, he was the center of attention.

In a precious memory recorded by his mother, when Richard was about three years old, he developed a strong fascination with the creek and enjoying throwing things from the little bridge. He tossed silverware and even a cream pitcher into the water. His mother recalled when something was missing they always checked the creek.

Richard's memories began after the family moved from the farm. He recalls living in several different upstairs apartments through the years. One such apartment was over the pool room and another was above the post office. But by far, his favorite upstairs apartment was over the bakery that turned into a candy store where R. J. Dove made some amazing candy bars. Dove had a device that coated the candy bars with melted chocolate. The candy would be sold to local small businesses. Richard still remembers when the smell of chocolate would waft upwards and fill the apartment. Later Dove added hot dogs for sale and finally he introduced frozen custard which was well received by the community.

Years later, as an only child with parents employed outside of the home, Richard found summer days long and boring. He had several aunts who lived in Broadway so he often spent time there. One day while walking along Main Street he saw his friend Bill's mother driving by. Bill's family had a farm outside of town. Richard had an idea so he called to her, "Can I come to your house?"

That was the beginning of spending every summer with the Martz family. Richard, the two Martz brothers, and a mutual friend named Pete would work hard on the farm doing whatever was needed and then they would play ball. They were all charter members of the local Little League with each boy on a different team. This fact made for a lot of competition and it seemed as though they were always arguing about something; but they were close friends and there was always something else to do. Those were his favorite times as a boy and they were over so quickly.

A favorite gathering place of the young people was the local theater. When they showed a double feature on Saturday nights the line for tickets would be over two blocks long, ending outside the drug store. Richard recalls many cowboys who visited through the years. He acquired a poster announcing Sunset Carson's visit. When Marilyn Monroe's movie "Some Like it Hot" came to town, patrons had to be eighteen years old to enter.

After high school Richard worked at the Riggs National Bank in Washington, DC, but he missed the country life. He fulfilled his military service in the Army and returned to the Valley. At a dance he noticed a beautiful young lady, Fonda Heatwole. She was still in high school, so he had to find someone to ask her if she would consider dating him. He was relieved to get a positive response.

In 1963 Fonda still had a year before she would graduate and that goal would not change, but they were in love so they planned to elope. They choose Hagerstown, Maryland because a blood test was not required there and they could get married in forty-eight hours after acquiring a license. Like many couples who choose to elope, they soon realized that the ceremony was the easy part compared to returning home to tell the parents.

Another complication was that Fonda had been registered as a contestant in an upcoming beauty pageant for single ladies. In the end they did tell their folks but did not announce publicly until after the pageant.

Richard worked at the Lee plant as a garment cutter. Standing on a concrete floor all day, he would perform the tedious task of cutting through a stack of fabric following the pattern perfectly. Just one error would affect the entire stack of material. When their first child a daughter was born, he decided he needed to get a better job.

He attended James Madison University, graduating magna cum laude in accounting followed by passing his CPA exam. This career change would eventually result in forty years as a CFO and Vice-President of a large company in the apple industry.

JoAnn "Cromer" Gordon

JoAnn grew up in a small community known as Spring Creek near Bridgewater, Virginia. She was the sixth of thirteen children. The birth order was four girls, a boy, then JoAnn, followed by three boys and finishing with four younger girls. JoAnn says being born in a series of boys, resulted in her being quite the tomboy. She loved sports and was an avid basketball and softball player.

One special Christmas memory she recalls the children received a bike to share. The older children learned to ride first; the younger ones would learn later. It was a well-used bike and the children quickly learned how to patch a tire. The few dolls they had were handmade by their busy mother. She used cotton material for the body and head then embroidered a simple face and hair on top. As the older sisters outgrew this pastime, they kindly presented their doll to a younger sister.

When the sisters were old enough to be employed outside the home they were able to buy clothes from the store. Sometimes a younger girl would "borrow" a skirt or blouse, being sure to return it quickly before her sister arrived home from work.

One sister worked at the Celanese factory and years later JoAnn joined her there. They worked the night shift from eleven to seven. JoAnn's task was to take man-made fibers from large cone-shaped bobbins, usually one white and the other colored, and twist them together by hand. The next worker would steam it to set it in the twisted shape. After it was set it would be placed on another bobbin ready to be woven into a special fabric. During World War II they received silk which they processed in a similar way to be used in the manufacturing of parachutes. Another portion of silk would be used to make men's ties.

She married Roy Gordon who was a carpenter and then later worked as a long-distance truck driver. With a large supply of siblings and aunts, she never had trouble finding a babysitter for their children.

The American Cellulose and Chemical Manufacturing Company was founded in New York City in 1918 by Camille Dreyfus. The first manufacturing plant was in Cumberland, Maryland and production began in 1924. In 1927 the name was changed to Celanese Corporation of America. It was a source of cellulose acetate commercial fabrics and yarns.

Hilda Rhodes

Looking back, Hilda didn't know what she was thinking when she planned to get married the Saturday before Easter. She assumed that her father would take care of the flowers since he was an excellent florist. But when she asked him, he told her it was impossible. The Saturday before Easter was the busiest day of the year. That weekend he would be working overtime to fill all the orders. Hilda tried to decorate it another way but finally gave up. When she stepped inside the church on her wedding day, she could hardly believe her eyes. Her father had come in late after work and had transformed the sanctuary with his beautiful floral arrangements. Hilda will always be grateful for the sacrifice her father made.

Hilda met her future husband, Gilbert Rhodes, who worked as a salesman in his family-owned business called Rhodes Candy Company. Traveling from store to store he would introduce their many candies and snacks. Eventually, he wanted to add other products like shampoo and toothpaste. With the family's blessing, he went into business for himself and named it Dominion Sales.

Hilda found employment in the business office of the telephone company in the Harrisonburg Telephone Company. She worked in billing and also took applications for people who wanted to have a phone installed. It was during World War II and if someone wanted a phone they had to apply for it, and their name was put on a list. Priority was given for those who worked in certain fields, like in a hospital or with the government.

In rural areas, the farmers had established an association for telephone service. This was the era of the old wall phone with the crank on the side to summon the operator. When the operator answered, she would ask for the number of the person one was calling, which was just a four-digit number at that time. Hilda recalls that Line 26 was a party line for farmers. There was any number from four to eight phones on a party line. The different ring tones would determine which party should pick up. It was apparent early on that due to error or just curiosity other parties might pick up and one's conversation would not be private.

During the War, just because you had the money, did not mean you could buy certain items. Many common items were rationed like canned goods, meat, sugar, coffee, cheese, butter, and gasoline. Some were restricted because they were no longer easily available and others were needed for the war effort. At the grocery store, the customer was required to have a ration ticket available for the item they wished to buy. There was a lot of wheeling and dealing with friends and neighbors since you could swap a ticket you didn't need for a ticket you needed more.

Sometimes a store would receive an order of something special like bananas, and the owner would offer a couple each to his best customers. These items were not on display. In that day, the customer would give the grocer or clerk a list of items and they would be chosen for you. If you were fortunate to have access to a phone, you could call an order in and it would be delivered to your home.

If you wanted to purchase a car or rent an apartment, your name would be put on more lists. She recalls at one point the dealerships only received a couple cars a month. As Hilda put it, "We learned to wait for things."

Mildred Kennedy Cromer

Mildred's father, Howard Kennedy, was the local blacksmith. He later turned to carpentry and was employed to build houses in the area. He even built a house for his family in the little community of Mayland, Virginia. Howard was trained in masonry as well. But his love for working as a blacksmith never died. Often after work and on weekends, he would be found in his shop sharpening tools, or at the forge repairing items. A simple sketch of a special item needed would be enough to inspire him to make something for a neighbor or friend.

When Mildred was in middle school there was a fad in which one purchased in a small kit with a tube of a thick plastic substance and a short, thin plastic straw. First, a small glob of the plastic goo was applied to the end of the straw. Then one blew slowly but steadily through the other end to produce a plastic bubble. After the bubble was carefully removed from the end of the straw it could be bounced around in one's hands without breaking. It was novel because the usual soap bubbles only lasted seconds. Mildred was so fascinated that she left school without permission to go to the drug store to buy some. When she tried it, it failed to work for her and she was very disappointed. She said, "When my parents found out that I had left the school, it sure wasn't worth it!"

Her first employment took place in Timberville, Virginia, at a business called "Dinner Ready." With chicken purchased directly from the local processing plant, the workers seasoned, cooked, and shredded the meat. The finished meat was packed in tin cans and sealed. They also prepared a popular item called chicken loaf, which consisted of dark and white meat tied in a bundle that was smoked in a smoking room overnight. In the 1950s, this was a very new concept of selling food that was prepared ahead.

Mildred also worked at The Return Motel located on Route 11 in New Market, Virginia where she worked with other ladies in housekeeping. One day they entered the laundry room to the sound of hissing. The noise was coming from a large barrel and peeking in timidly, Mildred discovered a mother opossum with her litter of babies. Apparently, it had fallen into the barrel and delivered the babies and could not climb up the smooth side. Two ladies carefully dragged the barrel outside with the frantic opossum hissing and baring her teeth. They tipped the barrel gingerly away from them and the mother opossum escaped with her little ones.

Her caring personality was a perfect fit for her longest employment at a senior healthcare facility. She started work at Life Care Center, also in New Market, from its first year of opening and continued for thirty-one years until her retirement. Beginning as a Certified Nursing Assistant, she then transferred to the Restoration Care, now referred to as the rehabilitation center, or rehab.

The Old Men of Timberville

Most seniors can recall the picture of two gentlemen playing checkers in the general store by the old wood stove. Another familiar scene from old TV shows included two or three men sitting on a wooden bench conversing outside a local business on the main street. We all loved Floyd's Barber Shop in Mayberry and the cluster of men sharing local stories and tidbits of what was new in town.

Beverly Garber grew up in Timberville, Virginia. His father was 54 years old when Bev was born. This fact might have contributed to his sensitivity to the dozen or so old men who wandered the streets of his town during the 1950s. But it was far from the Hollywood version. According to Bev most of the men kept to themselves and had one thing in common; they didn't like kids. One elderly retired teacher was particularly one to avoid.

In all fairness to the men, most of them weren't enjoying their golden years. Living on a meager income, if any, they had to deal with a few local boys who harassed them by calling them names or even stealing a man's clothes while he was taking a much-needed bath one early morning in the creek. Bev recalled one man who, after an encounter with one such bully, chased the lad through a ball field while a game was in progress and out the other side disappearing into the woods. The kid ran a safe distance ahead of him but it certainly left a lasting memory for everyone attending the game. Another time, a kid hollered something to a man across the street. The man picked up a rock and threw it missing the kid but breaking a large store window. Bev noticed the man later doing work for the proprietor, probably to pay for the window.

There were a few exceptions like a man who had a sports connection and would offer friends free tickets to a Redskins game. Another was a helpful watch and clock repairman. But most were like ghosts biding their time with no checkerboard to make it go faster.

In the evening they would wander off and disappear behind buildings into an old shed, a small trailer, or who knew? One man had a cot in a sheltered space below the local bowling alley. The shelter didn't even have a door.

In the winter a few would be invited to stay in someone's attic or cellar. On a cold stormy night, tucked in bed under his blankets Bev would wonder where the rest of the men were.

Norvell Preston Trumbo, Jr. 1923-2009

Growing up during the Depression, Brent Trumbo's father, Norvell, spent much of his childhood on his Uncle John's farm known as Myers Farm. It was located on the land now known as Walnut Ridge in Broadway, Virginia. When he was beginning elementary school, he had already learned to contribute during this time of bad economy. He collected black walnuts that grew on the farm property, shelled them, and sold the nuts for a few pennies.

In the fourth grade his teacher, Miss Burtner, expressed her creativity by introducing special class projects. One spring she spotted a lovely area by the playground southeast of the gymnasium. She envisioned a garden and only one thing hindered the plan: a large rock in the middle of the plot. Norvell and his classmate, JP Alger knew what to do. JP had seen rock removal projects on the farm and Norvell had connections. Norvell borrowed a hand rock drill and a sledgehammer from his grandfather and with Miss Burtner's approval, they started the work the next day. Each morning these two fourth graders with tools in hand would march out of the school to spend hours banging and drilling away at that rock. When they had produced a hole about a foot deep the teacher called for Sgt. Toby Long of the police department. The boys watched in delight as he poured black powder into the hole, tucked in a fuse and packed it with clay. Standing a safe distance away, they watched while Toby lit it and ran. Boom! It was an impressive crater soon filled with soil. The entire class worked hard to transform it into a lovely garden for Miss Burtner.

Brent recalls that Uncle John farmed with Belgian draft workhorses. Belgians were extremely muscular animals perfect for pulling heavy loads. The old barn had a hayloft equipped with a metal track and a pair of forks that hung down from the loft doors. The hay was loaded from the back of a horse-drawn wagon. From the loft Uncle John maneuvered the forks to grasp a cube of several bales of hay and hoisted it up into the loft. Then he would trip the release and the hay would be unloaded and stored.

John Myers also raised Ayrshire dairy cattle from Ayrshire in southwest Scotland. They were a hardy breed and were known for their easy calving and longevity. He sold milk until the farmers were required to pasteurize it. At this point, John shut down the business rather than comply, saying that it just didn't taste right after the pasteurization process. He also owned a cheese factory located near the old foundry.

Norvell founded Trumbo Electric in 1948, which actually began in a garage on the property. It is the oldest electrical contractor in western Virginia. He had a vision to fully integrate electrical engineering and construction into one business. Norvell believed that this approach would provide the customer with an electrical system of superior value. In the 1960s Trumbo Electric was the first contractor to employ engineers and practice design and build construction. With a deep desire for excellence, he developed a company that established the highest quality standards possible. He led the expansion of the company from a single employee to approximately one hundred employees at the time of his retirement in 1992.

Norvell and his wife, Doris, had three sons. Each son worked at some point in the company beginning as electrical helpers, but for Brent, the youngest, it was a natural fit. He graduated from Goshen College in Indiana and received his Masters degree in Business at James Madison University in Harrisonburg, Virginia.

While Brent was away at college, Uncle John's barn was destroyed in a fire. Though the barn was no longer necessary for business, Norvell knew how much it meant to John and rebuilt the barn out of kindness.

For eight years Norvell Trumbo served as councilman of the town of Broadway and two years as mayor, while also devoting many years to various church and community organizations. He will always be remembered as a gracious man of integrity.

Brent continued to accept more responsibilities as he grew in his knowledge of and experience in Trumbo Electric. He served as CFO and Human Resource Manager and then as Director and Treasurer. In 1989, he assumed the position of President/CEO. Through the decades he has diligently continued to connect with his employees and clients, securing the legacy of a business founded on integrity and excellence.

Tom and Dorothy Hawkins Moore

Dorothy lived on Central Street in Broadway within walking distance of the movie theater and rarely missed a show. Once, a cowboy named Wild Bill Elliot came to town. With his arrival, the theater announced a promotion that for just twenty-five cents one could have a picture taken with the actor and it would be mailed to one's address at a later date. Dot still remembers the long wait and the disappointment when it finally arrived. It wasn't even her in the photo! As she recalls, it was a boy standing in her place, so she threw it away.

Her Grandmother Hawkins was a petite and spry lady with an interesting personality. She was known to have pierced her own ears and also vaccinated herself against smallpox. Research showed that milkmaids who had experienced cowpox, a mild skin outbreak, were immune to smallpox. Cowpox, a disease which appeared on the cow's udders as ulcers, could transfer through a scratch or an abrasion on the milkmaid's hands. Grandmother Hawkins exposed herself to the cowpox. She also had a favorite saying that if it looks good, smells good, tastes good and doesn't make you sick, eat it. Apparently, this applied to other people's food as well. Dot recalls, "We'd be sitting at the dining room table with my grandmother seated next to my mother. Grandma was so shy that instead of asking for someone to pass the bread, she would quietly spirit a piece from Mom's plate."

Tom had a more isolated childhood growing up on a farm near the small community of Tenth Legion, just across the road from his grandparent's farm, which was known as Mooreland.

Aside from Tom's parents and his four siblings who lived on their farm, five maiden aunts and his grandmother lived on Mooreland. With most adult men from his family serving in the Army, it fell to twelve-year-old Tom to drive the tractor and truck for farm chores.

Tom's Dad, also named Thomas, would buy yearling bulls from West Virginia breeders or the local livestock auction, neuter them, and raise them until they weighed about a thousand pounds. A neutered bull, called a steer, was sold for beef. From May to August, the steer would graze on grass, but in the winter, they would be fed silage, ground barley, and cottonseed meal. Feeds and Feeding, a book by F. B. Morrison, contained helpful information about the properly balanced diet for animals and his father followed it faithfully. His Dad would sell about six hundred steers a year either to a broker for future delivery or as a last resort, he would ship the animals by railroad to Baltimore, Maryland.

His father was a graduate of Roanoke College and encouraged all his children to get a college degree. Both Tom and Dot graduated from college in 1952. Tom received a degree in Electrical Engineering from Virginia Polytechnic Institute, commonly known as Virginia Tech. Dot graduated from James Madison University with a Bachelor of Science in Chemistry. In this same year, Tom began work at the RCA Research Laboratories in Princeton, New Jersey, married Dot, and was drafted into the Army. In the Signal Corps Engineering Laboratories at Fort Monmouth, New Jersey, he was assigned to quality control for the many radios used by the Army in Korea: Walkie Talkies, Handy Talkies, radio backpacks, and jeep radios. His task was to test each radio and determine whether they met specifications.

Dot, a small-town girl, married Tom, from the farm and Tom proceeded to teach her to drive. However, his request for her to "whip over in the other lane" got her into a bit of trouble when she took it literally. Since then they have had sixty-six beautiful years together to work on their communication skills. Tom is not shy about admitting that he is married to the most wonderful gal in the world.

Wild Bill Elliott

Wild Bill Elliott, also known as Gordon Elliott, William Elliott, and Bill Elliott, was born Gordon Nance on October 16, 1904. Elliott grew up on a ranch in Missouri where riding horses was part of his life. Desiring to be an actor, he headed to California where he enrolled in classes and focused on his goal. After years of hard work and appearing in over a hundred minor parts, he finally had a break in his thirties when Columbia Pictures offered him the title role in a serial called *The Great Adventures of Wild Bill Hickok*.

In 1943, he starred in a series of westerns alongside George "Gabby" Hayes. The first film, *Calling Wild Bill Elliott*, gave him the name that would stick for the rest of his career. Later, Elliott landed his most renowned series called *Red Ryder,* based on a popular comic strip cowboy and his Indian companion, Little Beaver, played by the child actor, Robert Blake.

Wild Bill Elliott made the list of top ten western stars for fifteen years. His trademark was a pair of six-guns, or revolvers for us non-cowboys, which he wore butt-forward in their holsters. The last movies he starred in took place in 1957 when he was in his fifties.

After retirement, he was in the business of breeding and showing Appaloosa horses. Elliott came full circle, buying a ranch for his last home in Nevada, where he died at the age of 61 from lung cancer. Many of his films can be viewed on the internet today.

Frank and Ellie Mitchell

In the months before Christmas, Frank and his siblings would crack black walnuts and sell the nut meat. The pennies they earned were set aside for Christmas. Mother made all of his sisters' clothing and Frank remembers a special shirt she surprised him with.

Like the other children of that day, Frank attended a one-room schoolhouse. When he had a nickel, which was not very often, he would buy a bottle of Pepsi-Cola and tuck it into the cold water at the edge of the creek near the schoolhouse. At lunchtime, Frank would retrieve it and drink that ice-cold treat with his sandwich that his mother had packed. Frank's mother baked all their bread, and he is surprised when he hears of children who refuse to eat the heels of the loaf. When he was a kid, they would fight for the heels. Frank's mother was an excellent baker and when company was expected she would bake anywhere from six to eight pies in preparation for their arrival.

When Frank and Ellie were in school their sandwiches were always wrapped in newspaper. Ellie recalls, "When my mother packed a fried egg sandwich, the warmth of the egg would leave an imprint of newsprint on the outside of the bread." Of course, she ate it anyway, that was just the way it was.

The old Broadway Theater advertisements would include two or three names of local residents below with the ad. If your name appeared in the ad, you won a free guest pass to whatever was playing. It was always exciting to see your name or the name of a friend listed.

Frank's Uncle Otis and Aunt Hazel owned a home at the foot of Chimney Rock, a unique rock formation in Brock's Gap, Virginia. In the 1930s, it was a service station. When you purchased gasoline, Otis would write the transaction on a piece of paper and carefully tear it off for a receipt. He has a photo of a scrap of paper stating "Dave Turner, July 7, 1932 (for) 2 gal. Gas 42 (cents)."

Later, Hazel opened a homemade rug shop. She had two looms, one full-sized and a smaller one. As the business grew, she hired other women to work there. Others came to the store to learn how to make rugs. Ellie made a colorful rug of blues and reds which she still has in her home.

The Rug Shop at Chimney Rock

This is a recent photo of Chimney Rock taken from the opposite side of the former Rug Shop location. Today, trees obscure the view from the other side.

Photo of Chimney Rock taken by Retta Lilliendahl

Many seniors from the Shenandoah Valley remember the delightful couple, Otis and Hazel Mitchell, who lived near the base of Chimney Rock. In the 1930s, they owned a small service station which included a selection of maps and tourist items.

But Hazel had a passion for rag rugs and expanded her interest by teaching others the craft. Otis and Hazel called their store HEMWOM Weavers, an acronym derived from the initials of their names, Hazel Elizabeth Mitchell and William Otis Mitchell. There was an old Coke machine in the small entryway and beyond it a door opening to the rug making operation.

Photo of ladies in front of rug shop

Barbara (Dove) Turner began working at the shop when she was about thirteen. Travelers would often stop out of curiosity when they saw the shop name. Others would be drawn in by the Coke sign for a drink on a hot day. When asked about the rugs, Barbara would show visitors the shop and her current project. For her, it was always interesting to find out where they were from and sometimes the visit ended with the sale of a rug. Locals would bring rags cut into strips, attached end to end, and wound into a ball called rag balls. The two looms were both thirty-six inches wide, but rugs were ordered in any length. Hazel could look at the material and know how much was needed.

This photo shows Hazel on the left and Barbara Dove on the right weaving rugs on the looms.

Otis and Hazel had no children of their own. He worked for the state highway for many years which left Hazel alone during the day. For Barbara, working at the rug shop was like being with family. She and Hazel became very close. At one point, Barbara lived in the Mitchells' large house next door to the shop. She spent so many hours at the shop that it was convenient for her to be nearby. Hazel treated Barbara like a daughter. They even worked together in Hazel's garden and canned together in the summer.

One thing they thoroughly agreed on was the fact that they both *hated* snakes. Barbara recalls the day while working in the kitchen that she spotted what she thought was a black kitten's tail near the stove. Closer inspection revealed that it was the wiggling end of a black snake. She screamed for Hazel and Hazel's reply was, "I can not have a snake in my kitchen!" It disappeared behind the stove as quickly as Hazel and Barbara disappeared outside. They spotted a neighbor boy named Larry Tusing, who at that time had a broken arm in a sling. When they returned to the house, the snake was outside slithering up under the eaves. They knew they had shut the door so they suspected the snake had gotten out somewhere behind the stove. The boy located a fishing rod, and after making a loop at the end of the line, he flipped it up toward the snake repeatedly until he was able to lasso it. When he pulled on the rod, the line tightened around the snake and Larry yanked it down to the ground and disposed of it. Barbara and Hazel stayed out of the house until Otis arrived home from work. He discovered a hole in the wall near the stove where the snake had entered and sealed it tightly.

Otis had family and friends near Fort Seybert, West Virginia and he would go back occasionally to tend a cemetery there. Barbara recalls that it was a treat to be invited on the trip. She and Hazel would visit friends while Otis worked.

Arlene (Sonifrank) Miller worked at the rug shop for more than eight years. She recalls filling a shuttle with the rag material and weave it on a loom. Otis and Hazel were her friends, and when Otis could no longer drive, she would take them places they needed to go.

Ellie Mitchell married Otis' nephew, Frank Mitchell. Hazel taught Ellie to weave rugs in the shop.

This is a photo of one of the rugs she made. It is black, white, gray, and red.

Pat Turner Ritchie, a native of Fulk's Run, remembers her mother, Lena Turner, taking rag balls to donate to the rug shop.

Below is a photo of a rag ball that belonged to a member of her husband's family. It appears to be thin cotton-like dress fabric. Pat's grandmother, Ruth Turner, cut strips from pant material for a more substantial fabric. In that day, rags were recycled into functional rugs that lasted for decades.

Rag ball photo permission by Pat Ritchie.

All other photos in Rug Shop article used by permission from Frank Mitchell.

Lawrence and Linda Wilt

Lawrence and Linda met at Broadway High School. Linda recalls the first time she saw him; she knew he was the one for her. In his senior year, Lawrence heard about the Buddy Plan the military was offering, so he and a friend signed up together for the Marine Corp. The understanding was that they would serve together. But in reality, two signed up instead of one, and though they might have a rare glimpse of their buddy, they were on their own.

After boot camp, Lawrence and Linda were married. Whenever it was possible for them to be together, Linda joined him. They spent a year together while he was stationed in California. When he finished his service in 1964, they settled back in Virginia.

He had taken many college courses and several jobs before he began working as a building inspector with an engineering firm. It was this experience, which included learning the details and testing concrete, that proved beneficial for his life work. He secured a position as a salesman in 1976 with Superior Concrete. By 1979, Lawrence was co-manager of the company.

In 1980, the U.S. economy entered a recession which caused interest rates to soar, resulting in a decrease in business. In 1982, Lawrence purchased Superior Concrete. He sought ways to decrease expenses. Examining his fleet of trucks, Lawrence determined that ten of the total eighteen were in bad condition, so they were set aside. He was then able to save on maintenance by using parts from the trucks out of commission. Through careful management, the company was turned around. He has been grateful for the excellent work by his bookkeeper, tax person, and accountant, Kim Diehl, who has faithfully managed the business department since 1981. When James Madison University expanded and other businesses revived, Superior Concrete began to flourish.

Lawrence explained that people often use cement and concrete interchangeably, but they are not the same. Cement is actually an ingredient in concrete, which when mixed with water serves as a paste to hold all the components of concrete together, once the cement hardens. Concrete is composed of aggregates, which can include sand, gravel, or rocks held together with cement. There are eight different types of concrete; the ratio of the components determines the final product. The expression "pouring concrete" is not accurate, as it can not be poured, but instead it is "placed."

As technology changed through the years, Lawrence recounted some benefits as all measuring is computerized, making the process more efficient and accurate. The trucks are all equipped with GPS which allows the office to know their location at all times.

Lawrence and Linda have two sons, Tony and Keith, who both work for the company. Lawrence treated them as he did all employees. They began at the bottom and worked their way up. Each started as a loader operator, then spent time on the road as salesman and driver.

Today, Lawrence is the CEO of Superior Concrete. Tony is President and Keith is Vice President of Operations. The business continues to exemplify honesty, delivering a superior quality product on time.

Iron Furnaces

An iron furnace needed several essentials located nearby. Iron ore was number one, since sources estimate that it required about three tons of ore to produce one ton of iron. An available source of water-power was necessary to turn a water wheel that operated the bellows for a fire. A large supply of timber produced charcoal, the fuel for smelting the iron ore. The production of charcoal was an art in itself and required an experienced master collier, or producer of charcoal, with helpers who were dedicated to precision and care. Limestone, which is still in abundant supply in the Valley, was used as a flux, a cleansing agent. The limestone purified the iron by causing some impurities to separate from the ore.

Many of these furnace locations quickly grew into self-contained communities. They were called "iron plantations" and directed by an "ironmaster" who was well-trained in the process. The settlements included a house for the ironmaster, cottages for the laborers, tool and storage sheds. A company store sold goods for workers and their families. Stables were built to house the mules and oxen used to pull the wagons, the primary means for transporting of goods in that day. There was also a blacksmith shop where tools were made and repaired for the industry, wagons, and household necessities.

The first mention of mining ore in America was in 1609 when Jamestown colonists shipped some to England where it was declared ore of superior quality. About 1717, colonial Lieutenant Governor Alexander Spotswood opened the first successful iron making industry in the South called Tubal Works. It was located in Spotsylvania County, Virginia.

In 1781, Thomas Jefferson listed in his "Notes on Virginia" five furnaces that were in operation. Mossy Creek and Zane Furnace were the two located in the Shenandoah. By the 1800s, there were over a half dozen more in the Shenandoah Valley.

The furnaces varied in size, often thirty feet square at the base and twenty-five to forty feet high. The furnace was erected against the side of a small hill so the iron ore, limestone, and charcoal could be fed into the top by wagon. When the Civil War began in 1861, Virginia had fourteen charcoal iron furnaces in operation. Twenty-two others had been temporarily shut down.

When Virginia sided with the Confederacy, her most western counties seceded to become West Virginia and were loyal to the Union. This proved to be problematic since the Virginia iron furnaces helped supply the Confederacy with iron for everything from guns to cannons. They were now a convenient target for the Union forces. Liberty Furnace was damaged on more than one occasion, while the Columbia Furnace was burned three times, the last in 1864 never to be rebuilt.

After the war, many furnaces continued to produce iron. The iron-working jobs were strenuous and workers were provided room and board but were otherwise paid low salaries. Even after the building of a furnace by a conscientious owner, there were many things that could go wrong.
Transporting the final product to the buyers was costly and the early railroads were not always nearby. Another factor in the demise of the iron industry in Virginia was the competition in the north. Pennsylvania and Ohio were building iron furnaces that operated on anthracite coal which cut the costs of production significantly and Virginia could not compete.

The iron from these early Virginia furnaces was of excellent quality, less prone to rust, and stronger than some iron today. Iron stoves for cooking and heating, the frying pans that sat on them, and many farm tools were often passed down from generation to generation.

Thanks to Dale MacAllister, of Singers Glen, for sharing his research and for his review of this article.

Also, thanks to Oma Gail Simmons of Mt. Jackson, VA who graciously gave Retta Lilliendahl a tour of Jerome, VA

Lura Ritchie

Lura Ritchie was born on January 16, 1919, a time when mothers and midwives laid newborns on the open doors of woodstoves to keep them warm. Dr. E.B. Vaughn was able to help bring a healthy baby girl into the world, but unfortunately, Lura's mother died in childbirth.

Lura was raised by her maternal grandparents, Joseph and Fannie Strickler. She remembers her childhood as "one big recess" and her hometown of Timberville as "one big playground." Although president Woodrow Wilson was predicting another world war in the near future, and almost two-hundred thousand people had died from the Flu Pandemic, the prevailing gloom didn't affect Lura's carefree days. "I just did whatever I wanted to do. No chores, no responsibilities."

One of her favorite places to play was the "island" near the old Cold Storage where her grandfather worked (near the present-day Pilgrim's Pride processing plant). "I'd leave the house in the morning and usually didn't go back until it was getting dark. Nobody thought anything about it then. All of us kids ran all over the place. That's just what we did back then. Nobody was afraid of anything."

Lura met her future husband in the Timberville bowling alley in January of 1941, and they were married the following January. Although their love story was a simple romantic tale, the details of their wedding were a bit more complicated. Lura was in nursing school at the time, and her fiancé, Julius Ritchie, was scheduled to leave for service in WWII five months after the wedding.

To make matters more complex, Rockingham Memorial Nursing School did not allow their students to be married. "I would have been kicked out of nursing school if they found out Julius and I had been married," she smiled as she recalled the story.

Finding time to get married secretly was also a challenge. "Our schedules just didn't match! We tried and tried to find time we were both free. Finally, we decided that we'd have to get married during the hour break I had from nursing school." So, between 5pm and 6pm, the couple said their vows in front of Dr. Swayne in Dayton, Virginia and spent a twenty-minute celebration in -- of all places-- the Timberville Bowling Alley. Each then went back to their own houses and lived separately until Lura graduated from nursing school later in the year. But Julius had to leave for military service in June of the year they were married, so they didn't actually live together until after his discharge.

While he served in WWII, Julius wrote faithfully to his new wife. The letters were censored, of course, but he found an ingenious way of letting her know where he was stationed. He wrote the location of his camp on the upper right corner of the envelope, then placed a stamp over the information.

Lura passed away about a month after this interview. She left behind a beautiful legacy of 98 years of service to her family and her community. She is missed by all who knew her, but her stories and her kindness will always be with us.

Vallie May Stroop

Vallie May Johnson Stroop and her brother were the first "live" musicians on WSVA radio. Vallie May was six and her brother, Albert, was eighteen. Albert was a musician, and he bought guitar strings at Loewners Music store located across from the radio station. The owner of the music store had a brother who was an announcer on the radio, and he thought it would be a good idea to have some music on his show that was played directly in the studio. And so, a lifelong love of music was born for Vallie May.

She remembers standing on a folding chair to reach the microphone while her brother put his foot on the bottom rung to keep her from toppling over. They sang gospel songs they had learned from listening to The Grand Ole Opry.

When WSVA changed ownership in the 1950s, Vallie May says country music faded from the airwaves. But in 1961, she found herself back in the media performing bluegrass with Blaine Smith on what was then WSVA TV. The Show was called Shenandoah Valley Barn Dance and featured performers such as Blaine Smith, Buddy Starcher, Don Reno, and Red Smiley. She also was part of the Cactus Kiddy Club where local children were invited to come to the studio and sing.

Vallie May was born in 1929 in Timberville. Her dad worked at the local bank for a while, but he was injured in an accident while Vallie May was still a child. He was pulling down some trees when a horse fell on him.

In 1939, the family moved near Harrisonburg. Vallie May remembers looking out of her window one cold night in February and seeing flames rising into the sky. The Linville-Edom school was on fire.

Although the main building was completely destroyed, firemen were able to save the rest of the school.

Vallie May's dad always grew a large, community garden. During the hard times of post-Depression days, he invited the neighbors to come pick their "groceries" from his garden.

She was thirteen when she first met her future husband, Sydney "Spike" Stroop, also a musician. Vallie May was at a dance with her parents at Shenandoah Caverns (WSVA sponsored the music). She saw him again later on at Uncle Tom's Park near Orkney where she recalls picking a thread from his tie right before he and his singing partner, Buck Ryan, were about to perform. They got married some time later and formed a dynamic bluegrass duo: Spike and Vallie May.

Vallie May and Spike began playing music as a team when he came home from the Army when WWII was over, They were on WHBG for a time and then went to WSIG on the Saturday morning program. They perfored with Shorty King and Art Barret until 1960 when Don Reno and Red Smiley came to WSVA TV. They made regular appearances with them until Red's health caused a change in their band.

Spike and Vallie May started a Jam Session in Mt. Jackson at the old school house, then moved to the New Market Community Center until Spike became ill with colon cancer.

After Spike's recovery, they did a nine-year stint of music at the Timberville Community Center.

Spike passed away in 2010, but Vallie May continues the music tradition. She hosts the Spike Jam sessions at the Chimney Rock VFW Post 9660 every Friday night where they play to a full house.

Harry Long

Harry Long is pretty sure his mom could have run General Motors without a hitch. She was, manager, organizer, and sustainer of a nine-child family. Harry's father started out with high hopes. He had land, built a house, and began a family. And then, the Great Depression hit. He was deep in debt with no way to pay back the money. The family sold their farm and bought a home on a three-acre plot of land.

For one entire winter, his father sat around without a job. He knew that, despite nearly impossible economic conditions, he had to find a way to support his family. So, one morning, Mr. Long took the train to Washington D.C., and there he found a job working in maintenance at the Burlington Hotel. Since he was a skilled cabinet maker, he was able to find a better job as a cabinet maker for the National Institute of Health. He made desks, tables, filing cabinets, and any kind of furniture the department needed for operation. For eighteen years he worked in Northern Virginia, taking the train home every two weeks to visit his family.

In the meantime, Harry's mom took charge of the Homefront operation. She created a thriving produce business with her half-acre garden. She and the children made hotbeds in which they raised tomatoes, cabbage, peppers, sweet potatoes and other marketable vegetables. Harry recalls riding his bicycle to deliver plants to customers in Mt. Jackson. The Longs, charged twelve cents a dozen, and his mom always gave customers an extra plant for good measure. They also sold, tomatoes, green beans and lima beans to restaurants.

The Longs also had a cow, a pig, and some laying hens. They sold cream and butter and eggs locally. When Harry's brother Jim was thirteen, he found a job as a huckster's helper. The two ran a route in Washington D. C. When the man quit, Jim purchased his huckster route and delivery van. Since he wasn't old enough to have a driver's license, he hired a driver. They went from door-to-door selling eggs, dressed chickens, and vegetables.

The Long family didn't have electricity, so their only outlet to the outside world was the daily newspaper, the *Northern Virginia Daily*. When an employee of the newspaper came to collect the $1.50 for the year's subscription to the paper, the family had no money to pay him. But Mrs. Long, ever the shrewd business person, traded him $1.50 worth of Leghorn broiler chickens for a subscription to the paper. The man took the chickens to Mt. Jackson and sold them at Uncle Brack Myer's poultry business to get his $1.50 in cash.

One of Harry's least favorite jobs was to gather cabbage in the winter. The family stored cabbage heads in rows stacked next to the house. Over time, constant freezing and thawing would make the exterior leaves slimy, and not very pleasant to hold. Harry said that after the outer leaves of the cabbage were removed, though, the interior part of the cabbage was perfectly preserved and ready for cooking.

Harry and his family lived during what historians call the "worst economic downturn in the history of the industrialized world" – The Great Depression. They were willing to work hard, save everything, and use their business savvy to survive the hard times. They truly lived up to the adage, "Tough times don't last, but tough people do."

Odessa Dove Lantz

Odessa Dove Lantz had the life every little child dreams of: she grew up in a candy store! She even slept on sugar bag ticks filled with straw. Her father, Reuben Dove, was a candy maker who truly loved his craft! Although he took a course in candy making, he liked to experiment with his own recipes. Odessa remembers delectable candies such as peanut butter cream, coconut, and walnut cream flavors. At Christmas time, they made hundreds of coconut balls and dipped them into chocolate by hand.

Odessa's father was an enterprising man who knew how to market well. He always attended local baseball games and all-day singings with a car full of candy. So instead of waiting for the ice cream truck, folks followed the candy car! He also sold bulk candies to stores in West Virginia, Harrisonburg, and Broadway.

In the 1940s, Mr. Dove's candy was in high demand. During World War II, household sugar was rationed, and folks couldn't make the sweet desserts they loved. Because candy was his business, Mr. Dove was able to get all of the sugar he needed to make his sweet treats. By 1946, the candy business was doing so well that the Doves moved their store from the little building in Bergton to a store in Broadway.

Odessa's eyes sparkle when she talks about her childhood. She says she was "sheltered" from a lot of things that were happening in the world. She loved her home in Bergton, although, like many children of that time, she often had long, frigid walks to school. She remembers a particular time in second grade when she thought her fingers were frozen. Her teacher put them in cold water, though, and they "thawed" well enough for her to do her school work the rest of the day.

Odessa will always remember the magic of growing up in a candy shop. And although those days of handmaking candy are over, she still spreads sweetness with her smile!

The Longest Call

In today's world, we have instant communication at the touch of a button. Sometimes it's hard to imagine that less than a hundred years ago telephones were just becoming accepted as trustworthy means of communication.

A March, 1937 issue of the Harrisonburg Daily News Record reported that Harrisonburg Mutual Telephone recorded its longest call to date – a call from Honolulu, Hawaii to Timberville, Virginia.

Linden Orebaugh talked to his mother, Mrs. Pearl Orebaugh, his uncle, Dr. W. B. Fahrney, and his brother, Raymond Orebaugh all the way from his military station in Hawaii. The call went through quite a chain of cities to make the connection. It was transmitted from Honolulu to San Francisco, then to Chicago, and Washington D.C. Finally, it traveled from Washington D. C. to Harrisonburg, and then to Timberville.

Charles Moubry

Charles Moubry's family fell apart when he was five years old. His mother died, and his father sent Charles and five of his ten siblings to an orphanage in Timberville. Most of Charles's childhood memories revolve around the orphans' home – the shenanigans he tried and the tricks he played. Although his life wasn't easy, he always found time for fun.

He remembers Mr. and Mrs. Flora, the caregivers at the orphanage, as being strict disciplinarians. They often used sprigs from the apple tree growing nearby to punish misdemeanors. Even though the children got to choose their own switches, Charles wasn't happy with the arrangement, so he came up with a plan to limit the ready availability of the switches. He was one of several children who helped make the Sunday night ice-cream, and one day as he dumped the melted ice and salt, he saw a way he might be saved from further encounters with the apple tree switches. After each Sunday evening ice cream fest, he began to dump the salt water on the ground around the apple tree. Of course, his plan didn't work overnight. But eventually, his diligence paid off and the apple tree died. Although many wondered why this seemingly healthy apple tree grew frail and died, only Charles knew the reason for the demise of this switch-producing tree.

One Christmas, Garland, one of the children in the orphanage received a special gift: a carpenter's tool set. Charles admired the set from afar, but only Garland's best friend, Mark, the caretakers' son, was allowed to play with the toy.

One day when Mr. and Mrs. Flora, were away, Garland used his new saw to cut off a piece of the back stairs. Needless to say, Mrs. Flora was not happy when she saw this!

For some reason, Charles and his friend, Herbert Wheeler, were blamed for the damaged property, and Mrs. Flora whipped both boys. Charles and Herbert knew that it was really Garland who did the damage, but every time they told Mrs. Flora that they were innocent, she whipped them again.

Days passed, and once again, Charles figured out a way to get revenge. Now Mark had several pet rabbits. And Charles, after filling Herbert in on his plans, volunteered to take the rabbits down to the orchard to eat grass. Charles had some inside knowledge about the habits of rabbits. He knew that the rabbits would be in bunny heaven in the field, and that they would burrow into the clover for a long time, virtually invisible to the human eye.

After a while, Mark went searching for his rabbits. When he couldn't find them, he went crying to his mother. Mrs. Flora confronted Charles and Herbert since they were the last ones to see the rabbits. Charles told Mark that he would go get the rabbits if Mark would tell him mother the truth about the damage to the stairs. Mark finally confessed, and his mother sent him for a switch while Charles went to fetch the rabbits.

Charles got his driver's license at age 14 – a legal age during World War II. He had a milk route before school every day. Charles has continued to work hard throughout his life. Until recently, he planted a large garden and shared vegetables with the community. Although he has slowed down a bit, he still enjoys helping people – especially by sharing his delicious, homemade pies. He donates these baked goodies to fundraisers, special events, and occasionally to some lucky neighbor.

Although the stories Charles tells happened many years ago, he still has a twinkle in his eye as he shares the tales from his past.

Memories of Anna Harper

Many Northern Shenandoah Valley residents have fond memories of sitting at the counter of the old Broadway Drug Store. You could sit on the twirling bar stools and order a hearty, homemade meal for well under five dollars. But even more valuable than the food was the chance to swap stories with Miss Anna, the "drugstore grandma." Back in the late 1980's, I was fortunate enough to interview Anna for a local newspaper. That thirty minutes was probably the longest time I had ever talked with her. She was always bustling about cooking and serving. But for that half hour, she gave me her full attention and told me her life story in a nutshell.

Anna was short in stature but tall in stories. And she loved taking care of people. Her custom of nurturing folks began at an early age. She was the second oldest in a family of six and began helping out around the house before she was tall enough to reach the kitchen counter. In fact, she used to stand on a box so she could reach the table to knead bread.

She graduated from high school in 1931, and moved to Dr. S.L. Schuler's house on Main Street in Broadway. She spent seven and a half years as housekeeper for the doctor. She also worked seventeen years for Acker Black Walnut company in Broadway.

Her co-workers at the Broadway Drug Store appreciated her tradition of giving and caring for people. They called her an "unsung hero." Several of her friends sat at the counter as I talked with Anna. They were constantly adding comments such as, "she takes baskets of food to the sick; she's always giving somebody something."

Anna was also known for her straightforward way of speaking. "In other words," she told me, "if you don't want to hear the truth, don't ask me!" She said that she "had to tell the truth. I don't remember what I said five minutes ago, so I'm in trouble if I have to repeat it."

Like all of us, Anna admitted to building what she called "air castles." She even dreamed of having her own baseball team: 9 sons and a sixteen-room house! But even though life gave her a different reality—a small house and a dog—she lived a happy, relatively healthy life. She recalled only one close call: the accident of 1962. Someone had forgotten to tighten the lugs on her tires. The wheels ran off the car, causing it to flip and roll over seven times. Anna was fortunate to have escaped with only a few broken ribs. And of course, she was back at work the next week.

But time marches on. And even small towns such as Broadway experience the marks of change. The Broadway Drug Store is no longer on Main Street, and Anna has long since passed on. But Anna's memory will always live in the hearts of all who knew her.

Jon Gordon Smith

Jon Gordon Smith got an early start on life. He walked down the "aisle" for the first time at age six, "marrying" a fellow first-grade classmate, Miss Phoebe May (Orebaugh). Although the wedding was a mock wedding, the participants dressed in wedding clothes, carried bouquets of flowers and lined up in front of the schoolhouse. The "wedding" was a special performance for Miss Helen Garber, one of the teachers who was getting married. Jon remembers that he had to stand on a box so he would be taller than his bride! He still jokingly calls the ceremony his "first marriage."

Jon grew up on a farm and the family had to work hard for the food they put on the table. He recalls being part of an FFA program started by the Sears Roebuck Foundation to encourage agriculture development, particularly in Southern states. He was given a female pig to care for. Part of his responsibility was to breed the pig, care for her litter, and then pass along a young, healthy female pig to another person in need.

Jon's pig had twelve babies. He cared for the pigs until it was time to show them at the Rockingham County Fair, held then at the Linville Edom High School (now the location of Linville Edom Elementary School). On the day he was to show the pigs, he was unable to find a ride to the fairgrounds. Jon walked from his father's place of employment – Rocking-R Hardware in Timberville—to the Linville Edom High School softball field, a distance of about 10 miles. Needless to say, Jon was exhausted when he finally made it to the school. He arrived hot and tired, only to find that all twelve baby pigs had escaped from their pen!

He spent the next several hours rounding up the piglets so they would be ready for the fair.

Jon's family had a Saturday evening tradition that they kept for many years. The family would take eggs into town to sell to Jon Branner, a local egg packer. While Mr. Branner sorted and counted the eggs, they went to the Farm Bureau to buy their weekly groceries. After they finished shopping, they returned to pick up their egg money from Mr. Branner and then went back to pay for their groceries. The Smith children always hoped there would be money left over after they paid for the groceries because that meant an ice-cream cone and possibly a trip to the bowling alley.

Jon Gordon Smith "weds" Miss Phoebe May

Larry Dickinson

At age 12, Larry Dickenson and his friend, Richard Cullers lived every young boy's dream: they found hidden treasure! Although they didn't have to duel pirates for jewels or fight sharks for gold it was still a significant experience!

It all started when the boys made one of their frequent visits to Arvilla and Tuck Roadcap's apartment. The Roadcaps lived in an apartment above a building that originally housed The First National Bank of Broadway. The building was heated with hot water radiators, and Arvilla had asked the boys to go below into the bank area and make sure that the radiators were turned on.

The boys went to check the radiators (the bank was in the process of moving to a new building next door) and they noticed that the door to the vault was standing wide open! And not only was the door open, there was a box of money on the floor inside.

The boys were excited about their find, but knew they couldn't possibly keep the cash. So, they went upstairs to tell Arvilla about their find. Arvilla then took the boys over to the new bank to find the current bank president, Aubrey Moyers, and told him about the box. At first, he was skeptical, but soon found out the boys were telling the truth. He congratulated them on their honesty, and they all went on their way. Some days later, Mr. Moyers gave the boys two dollars each – a payment for their honesty.

During another summer adventure, Larry and his brother Carroll found an old, abandoned boat. The boat had a hole in one side, but that didn't deter their quest for adventure. They painted it black and wrote TITANIC in white letters on the side. They spent many happy hours navigating the waters of the North Fork of the Shenandoah using orange crate slats for paddles. The "Titanic" continued to serve them well until one day someone stole it. The culprit was never discovered.

Another adventure turned out a bit more painful for Larry. One winter day he went sledding with his church youth group. Before the sledding event, he "corked and waxed" his sled runners. This technique pushed the wax into the metal, making the sled runners as slick as glass.

The group met at the hill behind the Tom Fawley house – a prime sledding spot. When it was Larry's turn, he zoomed down the hill like a bullet – just like he had planned. Unfortunately, what he hadn't planned for was the bump in the hill. He hit the bump, throwing him over the sled and into a fence. Larry's head hit the barbed wire.

His brother and terrified friends carried him back to his house where his parents were playing Rook. Dr. John Glick made a house call and sewed up his lip. Larry got to miss school for several weeks while he healed from a concussion and the cuts and bruises of the sled wreck.

Larry and his contemporaries grew up in a carefree world—a world without video games, cell phones, or computers. Yet, adventures he experienced with his friends and family have created many warm memories – enough to last a lifetime!

Larry and his siblings, Kaye and Carroll at Christmas

Day Lantz

Day Lantz grew up by the rule, "if you didn't raise it, you didn't eat it." That was the mantra of many folks who lived during the Great Depression. Store bought food was scarce and families depended on big vegetable gardens, poultry, and livestock to get through the hard times. Day's father was a minister at the Damascus Church of the Brethren, and also ran a store. He worked hard to feed his family, despite a heart condition that plagued him his entire life. Day doesn't remember ever going hungry, but he does remember wearing shoes that were patched with old tire rubber. "Sometimes you could feel the nails coming through the soles," he remembers.

Day's first day of school in first grade ended up being his last day for the entire year. His teacher, Ray Emswiler, taught multiple grades in one room, and was busy with other students when young Day asked to go to the bathroom. Mr. Emswiler told him he couldn't go at that time, and that he should wait. Well, waiting wasn't on Day's agenda for the day. He decided that the most sensible thing to do was just do his business outside. In his five-year-old mind, that was a win-win situation: he could go to the bathroom without disobeying his teacher who told him he couldn't go to the toilet. Unfortunately, Mr. Emswiler didn't see it that way, and young Day was dismissed from school for the entire year. Eventually, Day was allowed back on school grounds, and he completed the rest of his school days on the right side of the law!

One of his favorite pass times as a young boy was to listen to boxing matches on the radio. Day's family didn't own a radio, but a neighbor, Joe Stultz, had one. Day and his friends would gather at the Stultz house to listen to the latest competition. Day's favorite matches involved bouts between Joe Louis and Billy Conn. In 1941, Conn gave up his championship title to Joe Louis in an epic match.

In addition to suffering from a chronic heart condition, Day's father walked in his sleep. His rest was often interrupted by these nocturnal meanderings, but he could not find anything that would keep him from sleep walking. One day, an elderly woman told him that she could cure him. Although the family doubted this old woman who smoked a corncob pipe could do anything to fix the situation, they agreed to let her try. First, she drew a picture of Mr. Lantz. Then she hung it up, and shot it three times. Nobody seems to know what kind of charm she performed with her drawing and bullets, but Day says that from that day on, his father never had another issue with sleep walking!

Day enjoyed playing baseball. In fact, he gained quite a reputation for being the best pitcher in the County League. Many weekend afternoons were spent on the baseball field. He made many friends, and all remember him as a wonderful baseball player.

He was drafted at age eighteen and went on to fight in World War II. Although he was with some of the first troops that came to occupied Japan, he was at home on leave when the bomb was dropped on Hiroshima.

Day and his wife, Odessa, still live near the place he grew up. They are both welcoming hosts to the folks who drop by. And you can be sure you'll always leave with a heart full of joy and a head full of stories!

Bea Reedy Fulk

When Bea Reedy Fulk says she had a long walk to school, she wasn't exaggerating. She and her two brothers had at least a mile trek to their two-room school in 'Genoa, Fulks Run. This particular walk was made more challenging because they had to cross a river by carefully walking on stepping stones. Bea remembers one particularly cold morning when she slipped and fell into the water. She said that her socks froze to her legs as soon as she got back out of the river. She ran back home and spent the day warming up from her freezing slip. When the water was too high to cross, the Reedy children had to take a longer route – this time through a cow field. Bea says she was terrified of the bulls in the field.

The little Genoa school she attended first opened its doors in October,1919, and faithfully served the families in the area for forty-two years. It finally closed in 1961 when the present day Fulks Run Elementary School was built.

Bea and her friend, Phyllis, were mud pie queens! They not only fashioned fancy cakes and pies from mud, they even iced them. They made a dough from flour and water and tinted it with food coloring and spread the colorful mixture over their mud pastries. The girls loved to play "house" with their dolls. Bea remembers a favorite doll that had an untimely end. She had a beautiful, porcelain doll she named Daisy. One day, for no apparent reason, she tossed Daisy into the air and let her land on the floor. Poor Daisy's head was cracked, and Bea was sad. To this day, she doesn't know what made her destroy her favorite doll!

Bea and Phyllis loved to cut paper dolls from catalogues. They created complete families from the Sears and Roebuck models. They made cars from lard boxes and took their families on wonderful trips around the yard. The Reedy children also loved to slide down tall hay bales carefully stacked by their grandfather. Needless to say, grandpa Ira wasn't thrilled to see his neat hay mounds scattered! But his anger didn't deter the children from their fun!

Bea's family was one of the first in their neighborhood to get a television. They could get only one channel, but she remembers faithfully watching her favorite T.V. show, Captain Video and His Video Rangers.

Bea now enjoys her retirement days in Broadway – a few miles away from her Fulks Run homeplace. And although she was terrified of the cows in the field on her way to school, she now collects cow figurines!

Bea and her husband, James

Mutual Cold Storage

Most youngsters only dream of climbing into frosty igloos in the midst of the summer heat. For young Bev Garber and his siblings, that dream was a reality– one of the perks of having a dad who worked in a cold storage.

Bev's dad was an employee of Mutual Cold Storage in Timberville for many years, and he always worked the night shift. During the summer months, Bev, his two brothers, and sister sometimes spent the night at the Cold Storage, watching their dad hoist 300-pound ice blocks with a hand crank, and occasionally venturing into the ice room, a place that rivaled Antarctica with temperatures of 40 below zero!

Mutual Cold Storage started as an idea in the mind of Mr. David H. Zigler. As all successful businesses, it began with a problem and an idea for a solution. . For many years, local apple growers had suffered losses during the harvest season because they had no way to preserve the crops—no place to store the fruit while waiting for buyers. So, in 1914, the enterprising young Zigler began his business venture by organizing a stock company and raised a capital of $20,000.

Money in hand, he then began to search for a building. It so happens that Mr. J.E. Strickler was looking to sell his Lone Star flour mill building, and the two men made a deal. For $5000 and fifty shares of stock, the building changed hands, and Mutual Cold Storage was born.

The first structure was built in 1914. The building was two stories high and connected by an overhead passage with the existing mill building. A small cooperage shop and a large packing shed were also part of the project. Growers hauled their apples to the shed for packing and grading until the first brick building was built in 1929.

Disaster struck in the form of a fire in November of 1918. But Zigler saw this misadventure as a chance to improve existing conditions. When the structure was rebuilt, the wooden floors were replaced by concrete floors, increasing the holding capacity to 37,000 barrels of apples.

The Mutual Cold Storage continued to expand over the years. Many residents of the Broadway-Timberville area have fond memories of the place – the huge chunks of ice, cool working conditions, and the constant flow of apple growers hauling their wares to and from the packing shed.

In 1954, Rockingham Poultry took over the plant and re-hired its employees. One era had ended and another had begun.

Bev still has great memories of his days at the cold storage – watching his dad work, sleeping on a little bench in one of the buildings, and rising at 4:00 am to catch some early morning perch from the dam nearby. All in all, not a bad way to spend a summer vacation.

Photo courtesy of Bev Garber

Judy Spahr

Judy Spahr started school much earlier than most of the children in her town. At age three she attended a private kindergarten with her older sister, Becky. Judy wasn't officially a student then, but Becky was afraid of the dog that lived at the house, and the teacher allowed Judy to come to class to help alleviate Becky's fears. Judy was a keen observer and a quick learner, and when the teacher taught the class words on flashcards, Judy learned them too. And so, by age three, she was reading.

Judy recalls seeing that kindergarten teacher years later, and the teacher told Judy that she had worried that early reading might have somehow messed up the natural sequence of her education. Judy assured her that she was fine, and instead of interfering with her education, the teacher had helped to create a lifelong reader.

Words and stories have always been a part of Judy's life. Her father owned a small newspaper in Kingwood, West Virginia called The West Virginia Argus. When Judy was older, she learned to type and proofread for the newspaper Due to the shortage of necessary materials during World War II, her father eventually shut down the newspaper. Also during the Roosevelt administration, her father was appointed postmaster for their town.

Judy was a teenager during World War II. Hers was the first class to graduate after the war ended. She was valedictorian of her class and was offered a college scholarship. She turned it down and moved to Florida to work in the private sector. A few years later, she returned to Richmond, Virginia and had settled down to work at a stock brokers office when the letter came.

The letter was unexpected and unexplained, but it was from the United States Central Intelligence Agency. After a battery of tests and interviews, she was selected to work on the U2 plane project – the plane that flew spy missions over the Soviet Union during the Cold War.

Because Judy had a big interest in politics, when she heard that John Kennedy was running for president, she left the C.I.A. and took a job on a committee working on national security issues and chaired by Senator Henry "Scoop" Jackson from Washington state.

During her years working on Jackson's committee, she met many interesting people. One event that sticks out in her mind the most is the day she shook hands with Alexander Solzhenitsyn. The famous Russian writer and historian was visiting the United States and was meeting with a group of Senators. Judy made sure she was in line to shake hands with him!

Judy left Senator Jackson's office in 1976 and worked with the Senate Appropriations Committee. She took early retirement in January of 1981 when the administration changed and Ronald Reagan became president. After she retired from the Senate, Judy worked with a public interest energy committee for several years.

She was visiting relatives in the Shenandoah Valley one weekend when she saw a "For Sale" sign in front of a charming townhouse in the tiny town of Broadway. Although she wasn't especially looking to move, the convenient location of the house drew her in. She bought the house and quickly became immersed in the comings and goings of the small town. She spent a lot of time volunteering for various activities at Village Library in Broadway. Judy considers her time at the library a highlight of her retirement. She also worked with other civic and church organizations, including the Plains District Memorial Museum.

Judy has done much in her long career, but through it all, she has kept her love of words. The joy of reading that was instilled in her young mind many years ago is still alive and well and waiting for the next good book!

Judy and Senator Henry "Scoop" Jackson

Judy shaking hands with Alexander Solzhenitsyn

Jim Branner

Jim Branner grew up on River Road in Timberville, that is until the flood of 1942 washed his neighbor, Franklin Wine's house away. After that frightening experience, the Branner family decided that it was time to move to higher ground.

Like many folks who grew up in Timberville, Jim has many memories of Miss. Lizzie Trussle—his first-grade teacher. What especially stands out to Jim is that Miss Lizzie was also his father's first grade teacher! She was strict, but fair, and most of the time the children stood in awe of her. But of course, children will be children. Jim remembers that Miss Lizzie always kept her lunch pail under her desk. Most of the time it was a relatively safe place to store her food. But once a brave (or foolish) boy ate her lunch, and another time, someone put an onion in it. Needless to say, Miss Lizzie was not pleased.

In another instance, Jim was using the typical, pre-calculator method of counting – his fingers—when Miss Lizzie caught him. She didn't appreciate this form of mathematics and promptly rapped him on the knuckles with a ruler. Jim learned a couple of lessons that day.

While students today have a school supply list half a page long, Jim's needs were quite a bit simpler. He remembers many school days when he used the same pencil the entire year. Jim also wore the same pair of shoes for the entire year during most of his school days.

One of Jim's favorite pastimes was listening to Gabriel Heater on the radio news. Gabriel was a radio broadcaster during some of the darkest times in United States history including the Great Depression and World War II. But even though times were dreary, the catch phrase with which he opened every show was, "There's good news tonight."

Jim's family also bought a 9-inch television set – an exciting piece of technology for the 1940s!

Jim grew up in a simpler time when a "word and a handshake" was a bond. He remembers hiking Old Foley Hill, trapping animals and selling their hides. Like many folks who grew up in the 30s and 40s, butchering day was always a big event for him. Year after year, Jim begged his grandfather to let him shoot the pig. But his grandfather never gave in. He told Jim that he was afraid the boy would miss and shoot the pig in the shoulder.

Jim enjoys retirement now, but his face still lights up when he remembers the "old, carefree days" when he was a child in Timberville.

Ruby Ennis

Ruby Ennis has many wonderful memories of growing up around her dad's store in Bergton. She was born in 1921 and she admits that "people have changed since back then." "Back then," a person's word was a bond, and folks sometimes paid their grocery bills with chickens, vegetables, or whatever they happened to have on hand. They also paid with rabbits, and Ruby remembers making the trip from Bergton to Broadway to ship them out for processing.

Her dad made grocery deliveries on Wednesdays. Folks would give him their orders on Tuesdays, and he would fill them and pack them for delivery the next day. Some of the most popular items they ordered were dried beans, white and brown sugar, and salt. Since most people grew big vegetable gardens and often had a dairy cow and other livestock, they bought only the things they couldn't get at home.

Although it has been about nine decades since Ruby started school, she still remembers some of her teachers—Miss Minnie May taught her in the early elementary grades, and Mr. Galen Wampler was her teacher in later grades. Students mostly packed their lunches, but in the coldest part of winter, the school provided hot vegetable soup. She remembers how good the hot soup tasted on those chilly days.

Although Ruby had a short walk to school, she remembers being afraid to pass a big, ancient white house on school grounds. She wasn't exactly sure what spooked her about the house, but she had nightmares about it on several occasions. She always felt relieved when she was finished walking by that house for the day.

When she was older, Ruby and her friends took an unscheduled "break" from school. Their friend, Warren Turner, had bought a car and he invited Ruby and her friends for a joyride at lunch one day. Ruby took the ride, but didn't bargain for the gas stop they made along the way – a stop at her dad's store! Ruby said she slid down in the seat and hid. As far as she knew, her dad never found out.

Medical treatment was scarce in Bergton during the 20s and 30s. Ruby remembers Dr. Caldwell and Dr. Moyer. Both were traveling doctors and didn't have home offices. They mostly helped with delivering babies and treating minor illnesses. Sloan's liniment was used as a cure for many ailments. Sloan's was originally developed to ease muscle strain in horses, but it soon became a source of relief for humans as well. Yager's liniment was also used, but Ruby didn't like the ammonia-like smell it produced.

Ruby has many stories to tell and enjoys talking about her childhood. She still lives in Bergton, surrounded by many of the same landmarks she saw as a child.

Susan Brown

When Susan Brown tells you that nothing much has changed at Bergton Grocery in the past fifty or sixty years, you can almost take her literally. If the old bench out front could talk, it would probably tell you the same thing. She says the one big difference in the merchandise is that they used to sell more bulk food supplies. Otherwise, things are much the same.

Susan grew up around the store. Her dad bought it from Bill Stultz, and Mr. Stultz bought it from Charles Souder. Susan's dad was also the postmaster, and the post office was conveniently located inside the grocery store.

The Bergton Fair always played a big part in Susan's life (and it still does!) Her father was president of the fair in 1953, 1974-78, and 1982-89. The fair used to look different than it is today. She remembers more exotic attractions such as elephants, and trapeze artists. Susan says the kids in the community would work all summer to have money for the fair – making hay and selling soda pop bottles. Even school was scheduled around the fair. Classes didn't start until the week after the festivities ended. The fair was like one big family reunion and everybody attended.

When you think of lawn parties and fairs, you think of hot summer evenings. That wasn't always the case with the Bergton Fair. Susan remembers one year when it was so chilly, folks had to wear big, heavy coats to keep warm. September in the hills of Bergton is not always mild! The Bergton Fair is still a big part of Susan's life. She has also been fair president, following a family tradition.

She still hangs out at Bergton Grocery too. In fact, she owns and manages it. Every day she is part of a family heritage that started many years ago: a comforting, steady place in a time of uncertainty and change.

Antique Cars and Trucks

Enjoy our collection of antique cars and trucks from the Shenandoah Valley! (Owners are listed below each photo.)

Sonny Smiley
1967 Chevy Camaro

Johnny Moyers
1967 Chevy Camaro

Keith Steckenfinger
1962 Texas Buggy

Margie Steckenfinger
1958 Meyers Manx Dune Buggy

Jeremy Turner
1947 Ford Pick-up
Jeremy is the owner of Maple Hill Restoration, Broadway, Virginia

Jeremy Turner
1965 Ford Falcon station wagon
Jeremy is the owner of Maple Hill Restoration, Broadway, Virginia

Ronald L. Kratzer
1940 Pontiac, custom 2-door sedan

1934 Ford Coupe
photo used by permission from owners Jack and Lisabeth Wenger, owners of WW Motor Cars & Parts, Inc. in Broadway, VA

Brant Halterman and son, Gavin
1965 GT 350 Mustang
Brant is the owner of Virginia Classic Mustang, Inc.
in Broadway, Virginia

Alex Neff's detailed replica of a 1916 Opera Coupe
Alex's story appears in Local Lore of the Shenandoah

All photos except for the 1934 Ford Coupe were taken by Retta Lilliendahl.

Kaye Dickinson Hill

In 1954, the deadliest and most costly hurricane of the season swept through the Shenandoah Valley of Virginia, and Kaye Dickenson Hill will never forget it. Kaye and her brother, Larry, were in school at Broadway Elementary when the storm began. Kaye was in first grade, and Larry was in sixth grade. As the storm grew stronger and winds increased, the school administration decided, for some unfathomable reason, that the children should be sent home. They told the "townies" – students who lived within walking distance to leave first.

To this day it's difficult to understand the logic behind sending children out into hurricane winds. We can only assume it made sense at the time! As the two children began to walk across C.D. Lantz's vacant field to their house, the rain and wind were horrendous. Larry and Kaye were both "puny, little kids" and she says "we took one step forward, but were blown two steps backward by the wind. If we had not held onto each other, we surely would have been blown away. We were soaked and exhausted when we finally arrived home." She adds, "That walk across the field from the school to home was the longest walk I ever took!"

The Crystal gas station in Broadway is also a big part of Kaye's memories. The station was located on the corner of Main Street and Broadway Avenue, just a few blocks from her family's house. Both her brothers, Carroll and Larry, worked at the Crystal and many of her teen friends hung around there. Kaye says she could tell whose car was taking off from the gas station and coming up the avenue just by the sound of the engine. Kaye also remembers taking six empty "pop" bottles down to the Crystal, and while there, she was often allowed to play a game on the pinball machine.

Kaye's church family was important to her as well. Before moving to the Avenue, the Dickenson family first lived across from the Broadway Methodist Church on Church Street in town. One of the church members – Mereta Landes – saw her and her brothers playing outside one Sunday morning. Mrs. Landes told them that they should be in church. Their mother agreed to the suggestion, and they began attending Sunday school and worship service every Sunday, as well as enjoying the Youth Fellowship and many years of Vacation Bible School with that church. They remain members of the First United Methodist Church even today.

Kaye has many warm memories of growing up in the town of Broadway. Having many other neighborhood children as friends, playing softball in their back yard, trick-or-treating, and enjoying an occasional milkshake at the drug store were an important part of her childhood.

Kaye and her brothers, Larry, and Carroll

Broadway United Methodist Church

When the first settlers came to Broadway, it wasn't long before groups of people gathered to worship. These first home congregations met at the Winfield house. In 1870, the Presbyterians built the first church building in Broadway and they shared the space with the Methodists. In 1881, the Methodist congregation built their own building on the corner of Church and Miller Streets.

The land for the church was deeded to the congregation by George Reherd, and the builders brought lumber from Brocks Gap by horse and wagon. The only stonemason in the area at the time was Cosmos Helbert, and historians presume he did the stone work on the foundation of the church. The first pastor of the First United Methodist Church of Broadway was Rev. Elias Welty, who also served other Methodist Churches in the area.

According to information released at the church's centennial service, (June 7, 1981), the United Methodist Church in Broadway was known for its elaborate Christmas programs. The church was decorated with ornate trimmings and the tree reached from floor to ceiling!

In 1970, the congregation built a new building on the Bluff between Broadway and Timberville where it continues to serve the community.

The Doc Dove House

The Doc Dove house in Criders was always known as the "haunted house." Although some folks reported seeing genuine apparitions such as disappearing dogs and ethereal figures, one of those "ghost" stories turned out not to be so mysterious.

Dennis Lantz remembers a story told to him by Leroy Siever. Mr. Siever, like many residents of Bergton and Criders, liked to spend time at the local grocery store telling stories and swapping ghost legends. One night, after an evening of tall tales, Siever was especially antsy to walk by the Doc Dove house on his way home. Apparently, the evening's stories had been especially spooky. But since Leroy lived on top of Shenandoah Mountain, he had little choice but to walk past the Dove house.

While he waited, hesitating to pass by the old house, a figure in white suddenly sped past in front of him. Leroy was terrified. He stood in shock for a few moments, and then, the figure ran past him again, and disappeared inside the house.

Leroy was so scared that he ran all the way up the mountain.

But in the light of day, his story took on a less sinister outlook. It turns out that old man Dove had an outside toilet across the road from his house. The ghostly figure in white was actually Mr. Dove in his long johns, running across the road to use the facilities and then running back inside his house! That time, the ghostly specter turned out to be quite human!

The Doc Dove House

Martha Crider Henderson

Martha Crider Henderson can't remember a time when art wasn't a very important part of her life. As the youngest of David and Marie Crider's nine children, she often found ways to include coloring and drawing in her daily tasks. At Christmas time, she and her sister always found coloring books under the tree. Martha quickly finished coloring all of the pictures in her own book and then taking her sister's book as well! She remembers using small stones to scratch images on to smooth, flat river rocks. And when her mother sent her to water the geraniums, she discovered that geranium petals made lovely ink when pressed on paper.

Martha attended Cootes Store Elementary School where her mother taught. And although she loved to color and draw, she didn't really get serious about a career in art until she moved on to Broadway High School. Her high school art teacher, Bernice Coffman, encouraged her to develop her art skills. In the 1954-55 school year, Martha designed the Gobbler logo and created the dogwood image that was used on BHS class rings.

Martha particularly remembers her adventures in Mr. Carlyle Lynch's drafting class. Up until then, no girls had ever taken drafting. She remembers going to Mr. J. Frank Hillyard, the principal at the time, to ask if she could join the all male class. She says she was "shaking in her boots" as she approached him. Mr. Hillyard laughed and said, "Martha, do you realize that you will be the only girl in a class of thirty boys?" Martha realized, and was perfectly fine with the idea!

During high school, Martha raised chickens for money to buy art supplies. When she finished high school, one of her sisters invited Martha to come live with her in Los Angeles. So Martha moved across the country to live with her sister and to attend Los Angeles City College.

Although Martha says that her degree in Commercial Art became obsolete "almost as soon as I left college," she continued to pursue her artistic passion. She moved back across the country to Washington D.C. to look for a job. She found a place as assistant director of the Mickelson Gallery. During her thirty-nine year adventure at the gallery, she met many famous artists and handled many works of art.

Martha and her husband, Floyd, retired and moved back to the Shenandoah Valley. Martha is still a prolific painter, accepting commissions and working on personal projects. Her house is a gallery -- a lovely testament to her lifelong creative passion.

Winky Dink and You

One of my favorite children's shows as a ten-year-old was a Saturday morning show called "Winky Dink and You." I remember sitting on the floor in front of my old Philco TV set and watching the little character with big eyes wearing a five-pointed-star-shaped hat as he got into situations where he needed my help. The host of the show, Jack Barry, told me to have my parents send for a special kit which included a magic screen so we could be part of the show. The cost was five cents and probably postage, which was very little back then. I asked my mother who said she would ask Dad. I waited, but nothing seemed to happen. I didn't want to ask Dad if he agreed because of his frequent comments. My Dad was pretty skeptical about ordering anything from the TV, and I recall him warning us when commercials came on saying, "That probably doesn't work! That looks like a cheap piece of trash!" and my favorite, "I could make one of those."

So, I finally forgot about the kit. Taking the last comment to heart, I devised my own magic screen by taping waxed paper on the TV and using my regular crayons to draw as directed by Mr. Barry, but it wasn't the same. I spent a lot of time erasing the crayon marks, and the waxed paper was temperamental.

Months later when Mother handed me a package, I was thrilled to open my very own Winky Dink and You kit. It included a cool-smelling green magic plastic screen, a magic cloth, and a small box of special easy-erase crayons. There were four colors: black, red, green, and yellow.

Just a few weeks later, the show ended abruptly. I never knew why, until I was recently researching and found that there was a public scare about being exposed to x-rays from the picture tube.

Another interesting detail I discovered was where the idea for this interactive show began. A company received several complaints about a commercial for Benrus watches. Viewers said though the price quoted was $39.95, one watch listed was much higher. The discrepancy came from the fact that TV sets varied in how much of the screen viewers could see. On some sets, the "and up" after the price was cut off. While troubleshooting the problem, Harry Prichett, a graphic designer, placed an acetate film over the screen so he could sketch the area of the commercial that was visible using a grease pencil. It dawned on him that this could be a unique way for children to interact with a TV show. That was the concept for Winky Dink and You.

From 1969 until 1990 the show was syndicated for sixty-five episodes. In the 1990s, a DVD program of Winky Dink and You came on the market with a kit that contained a screen, crayons, and eraser that worked with older sturdy TV models.

By Retta Lilliendahl

Take Me Out to the Ballgame!

Early 1950s Timberville ball team (photo courtesy of Jane Hoover Smootz)

(If you can identify any of the players, email names to trfcullers@gmail.com)

Retta Grace Cooper Lilliendahl

My story began in the winter of 1945 when I was born Retta Grace Cooper in New Jersey, more specifically, South Jersey. I grew up in Jersey's largest city by square mile, though most people in any other state have never heard of it. That city was Vineland.

I was the second of four children, with an older sister, and two younger brothers. Our family attended an Independent Baptist Church where my grandfather was the pastor, and my dad played the piano.

My sister and I attended a small private school until I completed fourth grade. At that time, we transferred to public school. I discovered on my first day of fifth grade as the math teacher introduced division that I was in trouble since I hadn't had multiplication yet. Dad made flash cards that went through the nine times tables. I wish I could say I that it came easy for me and I caught up with the class in a short time, but that would be a stretch. Let's move on.

My favorite childhood activity was playing paper dolls, mostly developing stories and especially dialogue for my characters. My life seemed quite isolated from the world around me so through my imagination I created my own circle of friends and my own identity. In my teenage years, I branched out to several pen-pals along the way. Relaying stories and daily life in an interesting way was fun for me.

Reflecting back, I could have been a wallflower in high school, if I had tried, but I never achieved that status. I graduated in a class of 365. I was so invisible I could have been a double agent, but my lack of geography would have eliminated me from the job. I remember one monumental day when I received an A+ for my essay titled "My Trip to Mars." The teacher said that I had a very good imagination. It was the only compliment I ever recall.

At twenty-one, I shared an apartment with a girlfriend from church. She had attended Prairie Bible Institute in Alberta, Canada for a year and had taken a year off. After a sudden decision to return, she convinced me to enroll, also. She fed me a line about how the school was known for its romances. Finding a Christian mate, sounded like a good deal to me since at that time my options were down to a half dozen pen-pals that didn't seem to be going anywhere.

When we arrived on the campus after a five-day car ride, I realized the word "Prairie" meant it was as flat as South Jersey minus the trees. It was a missions school with seventy-five percent of the graduates going into full-time ministry to places I couldn't find on a map if I had one. There were missionary children enrolled in the college and its high school as well. The staff was responsible for the students' welfare, and it showed in the layout of the school and the detailed handbook.

The cafeteria had separate entrances for male and female students with their own serving lines. A wide aisle down the middle of the room I nicknamed, "The Red Sea" but it never parted for me. Only God knew where the male student dorms were located. The only stores I recall in the nearest "town" was a tiny bakery, a drug store, and someone said there was a dentist office.

Our handbook made sure we never went there at the same time as the guys did. So I was back in school, lucky me, but this time we were studying the Bible and once I got over the shock of living in No Man's Land, I enjoyed the classes and completely forgot about my Plan A. Living in an atmosphere of acceptance, I had a new awareness. No one knew me, so I was free to become the person I always wanted to be and made friends.

Then something happened the last week of school that would change everything. I discovered that the wife of a staff member had been best friends with my sister's mother-in-law in New Jersey, before she moved to Canada. When you are three thousand miles away from home, that is like finding a close relative. So, I grabbed two friends and went for a visit. While in the house, a young man named Al showed up from Connecticut to visit their oldest son. A dozen people were in the house at that time and I don't remember a conversation with anyone. But Al noticed me and bought a yearbook that listed all the students' addresses. When I arrived back in New Jersey, I received a letter from him inviting me to his graduation from the University of Connecticut. I had to dig out a map to find Connecticut.

I must butt in here and say something about my dad. The first time Dad ever saw a VW Beetle, he declared that none of his children would every ride in one since it was obviously a death trap. Al showed up at my home in a red VW Beetle! The next day he was taking me to Connecticut five hours away. All I can guess is that Mother must have intervened.

When I returned from Connecticut that following Monday, I was engaged to be married. Long distance phone calls were expensive, but we both wrote often. We only saw each other seven times before we were married. After our wedding, we headed to Pensacola, Florida where Al started his military career in the Navy flight program.

We moved every few months for the first two years and every four years after that. I loved to travel, and my world opened up as we visited new churches and made new friends. Still an avid letter-writer, I was writing letters to family members especially my in-laws. My mother-in-law answered every letter quickly. It was on a visit with Al's family that his dad took me aside and encouraged me to pursue a writing career. He enjoyed my letters and said I had a way with words. Not long afterward, I enrolled in a two-year correspondence course on writing children's stories.

Later, while living in northern Virginia, I signed up for a writer's conference in Pennsylvania. On my way home, as fate would have it, I shared the train with a freelance writer from the conference who lived nearby. Both of us were spun up from the conference, and she offered a plan. If I would assist, she would found a writer's group in northern Virginia. I agreed and that was the beginning of NOVA Christian Writer's Fellowship. It was my first exposure to people in the literary world and I loved it. Writers spoke at our monthly meetings and we critiqued each other's work. The director started a monthly newsletter in which I wrote a column.

After a few years, my husband retired and we relocated to the Shenandoah Valley. In a very short time, I met Tammy Cullers at a writer's group at the local library. By then, I was totally in love with the Valley, and we realized the need to save stories from those who had grown up here. So, here we are, pumping out our third local lore book. I count it a privilege of a lifetime for me to have interviewed over one hundred amazing people for these books and to share their stories.

Tammy Fulk Cullers

When I interview folks about their lives and encourage them to tell their stories, most will say that they don't have anything interesting to talk about, or that their story is much like everyone else's. I always tell them that recording their memories is important, even if they don't think they have riveting tales to tell. Now, as I attempt to relate my own story, I understand how they feel. What could a fifty-something baby boomer possibly have to add to a rich collection of Stories from the Shenandoah? But, taking my own words to heart, I will attempt to share a few anecdotes from the life of a Fulks Run native!

In 1960, the average house cost around twelve thousand dollars, bread was twenty cents a loaf, and Harper Lee published her classic novel *To Kill a Mockingbird*. In a little town in the heart of the Shenandoah Valley, a teen-aged woman and her twenty-one-year-old husband gave birth to a little girl.

I sometimes still wonder if they didn't find me beneath a cabbage leaf or tucked under a mushroom cap. I am so different from the rest of my family. But I have my dad's eyes and nose, and my mom's resilience and sense of humor, so I guess I belong.

They named me Tammy after the character that Debbie Reynolds played in the movie, *Tammy and the Bachelor*. Mom and Dad both used to sing the song "Tammy" to me—I think it must have been the movie's theme song.

I was a very fortunate child in many ways – I had strong family connections, parents who loved me, and most of all, a mom who read to me. Not just bedtime stories or naptime tales. She read to me almost every day from morning till late afternoon. As long as I requested another story, she obliged. Because of her intense dedication to sharing words with me, I learned to read for myself at age three. I also began to create imaginary worlds peopled with eccentric folk and talking animals. Mom played these story-games right along with me (she often tells me that she and I "grew up together"). All day, every day, my mind was filled with words. They still are.

My dad was the pastor of a small Independent Baptist Church, and I began playing piano there at age six. Granted, I just picked out the melody with my right hand and played cords with the left hand, but it was all they had, and we got by. As long as they could sing in the keys of C, F, or G, we were in good shape!

One day I was practicing piano with the screen door propped open. I felt an uncanny sensation—a tingly feeling as though someone- or something- was watching me. I turned around to see a large black snake curled on the welcome mat. I screamed, and my dad came running. Of course, when he got there, the snake was gone. But I was adamant that there had been a black snake at the door, so Dad searched the place from top to bottom. Eventually, he found the critter curled up in a 16mm movie projector. The tale did not end well for the snake, I regret to say.

Being a preacher's kid had its trials – especially in a tiny town. I don't think I was a particularly good kid – I just learned how to be stealthy! I was an only child, and any story that was told about that "Baptist preacher's kid" was about me. So, I had to be careful not to do anything story-worthy – at least under the scrutiny of the church parishioners!

My grandma was born in 1899, so her stories had a charm all their own. Her parents spoke mostly German – or Pennsylvania Dutch as they called it. Most of her siblings survived to adulthood, but I was fascinated by her story of little Gertie—the little sister who died at age three. Grandma always said that Gertie was too beautiful for this world. Her eyes were wide and blue, and her hair hung in golden ringlets. I don't know what illness took Gertie, but her ghost – in the form of my grandma's stories –haunted me for many years.

Grandma's brother Isaac (Ike) was called to serve in World War One when he was just eighteen. He had never left the hills of Bergton until he was summoned to fight for his country. He died in France several months after he enlisted. He is buried in France, a continent away from the rest of his kin.

I feel fortunate to have grown up surrounded by a loving family. I suppose we were rather poor, living for a while on the tiny salary the church folks could afford to pay my dad. We ate a lot of beans, potatoes, and rice pudding, but we had enough. Friday evenings were grocery evenings, and we had special indulgences: bar-b-que potato chips, Reece Cups, and Dr. Pepper! What a treat!

College, marriage, and children took me on different adventures, but those tales are for another time. In the scheme of captivating stories, mine is on the uneventful end of the spectrum. But life is good. I have never lived far from my hometown. Although education and travel has given me a broader outlook on life than I might have had without them, I still live close to my roots. I teach in my old high school (now a middle school) -- the same school my parents, husband, and children attended. I still play piano in church (I use a few more notes now than when I was six!), and I continue to enjoy listening to tales of the past. Most of all, I still have an enormous love for words and stories – a legacy that will always be with me.

World War II Observation Tower

World War II affected the Shenandoah Valley in a lot of ways. Even folks in small towns such as Broadway had to change their lifestyles to accommodate the war effort. In 1942, the Town of Broadway built an observation tower on a hill that overlooked 259 just off Broadway Avenue. The tower stood on a platform about 20 feet above ground.

The site had been chosen by the U.S. Army and approved by the State Aircraft Warning Service as a part of the east coast air patrol. Its mission was to spot any unidentified aircraft which might have gotten through the air defense system

Mrs. John Holman Kline served as a chief observer, assisted by E.W.Roller, Mr. J.E. Williams, Miss Lennis Moyers, Mr. J. Frank Hillyard, and Mrs. Herman Hollar.

The observation tower now sits beside the Plains District Memorial Museum in Timberville.(information from the Plains District Memorial Museum)

Jump on the Bandwagon

In the early 1900s, Timberville town residents could see the director, Dr. W. B. Fahrney, and members of the Timberville Brass Band riding through town in a brightly colored wagon, drawn by several horses.

The Timberville band was organized in 1879 when almost every little town had a brass band. But by the end of World War I, the Timberville band had diminished to just a few members. Musician Harry Bull and Dr. Fahrney set about rebuilding the band. The band played for lawn parties and events all over town, and was quite popular in its heyday in the 1930s and 40s.

Now, the bandwagon sits in the Plains District Memorial Museum bringing back memories for everyone who passes by.

The Bandwagon in it's "forever home" at the Plains District Memorial Museum in Timberville

The Outdoor Shop

One of the icons of the town of Broadway was Marvin Showalter's Outdoor Shop. Many generations of local folks remember going into the Outdoor Shop, talking to Marvin, and marveling at the way his shop was put together. To the average observer, the place looked like a hoarders delight with little rhyme or reason to its organization. But Marvin knew exactly where everything was located. He might sigh heavily and look as though you just might be ruining his solitude when you asked to buy an item, but he would walk slowly through the narrow aisles, push away dust-covered boxes and find exactly what you were looking for.

Unfortunately, Marvin passed away before I had the chance to interview him, but I did an informal Facebook poll about Outdoor Shop memories. Here are some of the responses I got:

--Being a kid on a bicycle and being a little bit afraid to buy tennis balls there...

--Marvin would hang out in the barber shop and periodically look out the window for potential customers approaching the store. There was a generic catalog bearing the store's name in the barber shop magazine rack, but he would sometimes sell an item for the price he marked on it in 1963 (if he could find it).

--I loved going there as a kid. My dad would go there to loaf around with Marvin and take me along. The shelves were packed so full, tight and high it felt to me like it could fall over on me. Marvin always knew where everything was. I don't ever remember him smiling even though I really liked him!!!

--Big sigh...
Converse Chuck Taylor All Stars.
My first nice new ball glove.
My first Louisville Slugger 30" bag.
My first real regulation softball.
My first tennis racquet.
Crowded aisles.
Wonderful memories.

--I remember wondering what was in there but not being brave enough to go in!

--My first ball glove which I still have. Buying Joe's Flys fishing lures for .99 cent when they were 1.50 at KMart. Marvin huffing and puffing. The stuff literally falling off the shelves.

--Walking sideways thru the aisle as a kid. Dunno how any adult fit. Marv huffing and puffing like a freight train.

--Ohhhh and buying .22 shells for .50 cents a box and Marv always saying. You can't shoot these in a pistol, because at that time you had to be 18 to buy pistol ammo.

--The smell of old wooden floors! Never crowded but always had what a country kid needed... bait and ammo.

--We would walk past it all the time but never go in. I think I bought fishing line there once. Always handwritten signs in the windows.

--One visit for tennis shoes; asked Marvin if he had a certain size. He breathed in and by the time he let that breath out, he said, " I think I do." Took off for the back of the store and came out with the right shoe. My dad called him " wheezer". I don't remember ever seeing him smile, either, but he was always so friendly. Nice man!!

Conclusion

Tammy and I published our first local lore book, *Regards to Broadway, the Story of an American Town,* back in 2005. It was from a desire to save stories of seniors who grew up in Broadway, Virginia and to collect a little history of our town. Most of the forty-seven people we interviewed at that time have passed on. Saving those stories made a significant impact on our community and even ourselves.

In 2007, we published our second book, *Local Lore of the Shenandoah,* which included a brief history of each town and interviews from seniors who grew up in Broadway, Timberville, New Market, Linville/Edom, Singers Glen, Bergton, and Fulks Run. This experience increased our knowledge and love for the Shenandoah Valley. The feedback we received from our readers was, once again, positive.

This final book in our local lore series includes interviews from all over the Shenandoah Valley. Saving stories is rooted in our hearts. We trust that these glimpses back in time will be both a blessing and informative to our readers. We hope that it will cause families to take time to record their own recollections while there is still time.

Retta Grace Cooper Lilliendahl

Made in the USA
Middletown, DE
16 March 2019

Stories from the Shenandoah

Photographer: Katie Cullers (katieleaphotography.com)

Graphic designer: Alfred C. Lilliendahl

The photo on the cover is of the old spring house in Frog Hollow, Virginia. The log structure straddles a branch of Joe's Creek on land belonging to Larry Gray.